CHRISTIAN ETHICS
IN THE WORKPLACE

CHRISTIAN ETHICS IN THE WORKPLACE

Raymond L. Hilgert

Philip H. Lochhaas

James L. Truesdell

CPH
SAINT LOUIS

Copyright © 2001 by Concordia Publishing House. Published by Concordia Publishing House, 3558 S. Jefferson Ave., St. Louis, MO 63118–3968. Manufactured in the United States of America.

Library of Congress Cataloging-in-Publication Data

Hilgert, Raymond L.
    Christian ethics in the workplace / Raymond L. Hilgert, Philip H. Lochhaas, James L. Truesdell.
        p.   cm.
     ISBN 0-570-05299-8
        1. Christian ethics. 2. Business—Religious aspects—Christianity.
I. Truesdell, James L., 1949-   . II. Lochhaas, Philip H., 1924-   . III. Title.
    BJ1251 .H55 2002
    241′.64—dc21   2001002878

1 2 3 4 5 6 7 8 9 10   10 09 08 07 06 05 04 03 02 01

Contents

Christian Ethics
in the Workplace

Foreword

A nd whatever you do, whether in word or deed, do it all in the name of the Lord Jesus, giving thanks to God the Father through Him" (Colossians 3:17).

Before He began His active ministry, Jesus was an employee of a small family business. He and His father, Joseph, operated a carpentry shop, where they doubtless experienced the same kinds of problems we face in our daily work lives. There were tools to be maintained, customer deadlines to be met, fair prices to be established, returned goods to be dealt with, and material suppliers to be paid. When He gathered His disciples, most of them also came from various small business backgrounds.

Work and career were established parts of life for Jesus and His followers—including a number of commercial fishermen—before they turned to the great mission at hand. They had experienced all the best and worst that working for a living could bring, and they probably had come to learn that some people could be trusted to carry out commerce in an ethical way and others could not. That same division exists today. There are individuals and companies who approach their task within an ethical framework, and there are those for whom expediency and self-interest are the only guides. Sometimes it seems that the Christian trying to compete in the world is fighting with one hand tied behind his back. "The Bible is fine for Sundays," people say. "Ethics are great for academic discussions. But if we had to follow these rules in the working world, we would soon be out of business."

Often we as Christians are faced with this dilemma. The business world appears to be a dog-eat-dog, adversarial environment in which self-interest rules and one is either a winner or loser. It just does not fit with the messages we have received in church, from Scripture, and from Christian tradition. The concepts of loving our neighbor and putting others' interests before our own seem to be a prescription for failure in the workplace, whether we are employees or business owners. We often compartmentalize our faith as something that just cannot be applied to our job. This forces us to lead a double life whereby we live by Christian principles in our dealings with family, friends, and the community, but adopt a different standard of behavior in the workplace. While this compartmentalization is a source of great internal conflict for some, it is distressing that so many professing believers see no inconsistency and, in fact, take pride in their tough, adversarial approach to the work world.

The goal of this book is to resolve this dichotomy

and provide some practical guidelines for the believing Christian to successfully blend faith and work life. The authors all share an interest in the study of ethics and moral behavior as it relates to business and the work environment. All three of us—a pastor, a business school professor, and a business executive—are members of St. Paul Lutheran Church in Des Peres (St. Louis), Missouri.

Along with several other knowledgeable laymen, we conducted two adult Bible study classes in 1996 and 1997, blending our knowledge and understanding of biblical teaching with practical knowledge and experiences. The success of these class efforts, coupled with a number of presentations and seminars at other congregations and forums, convinced us of the need to develop our material into a book and instructional package that could be of interest and value to Christian people who struggle with ethical applications in their business and workplace lives.

Running throughout this book is the belief that Christian life is not something that can be compartmentalized, but rather must be manifested and demonstrated whenever we interact with other people. Unfortunately, there are those predatory individuals we run into who will perceive adherence to morality and ethics as a sign of weakness (though it is, of course, the opposite) and will take advantage of those who make themselves vulnerable by acting with trust toward others. This is just one example of numerous conflicting areas that can be

11

baffling to Christians in the workplace. Although from a biblical perspective there are right and wrong choices, many workplace decisions seem to be very gray in their outcomes and Christians often are confused by contradictory pressures concerning what should be done. For this reason we will point out scriptural teachings, as well as supply practical suggestions and guidelines for making more ethical choices.

We believe that Christians must truly affirm their commitment to Christ by showing in the workplace that decisions and actions indeed reflect the teachings and examples of God's Word. While the main focus here is on ethics, that is, good works, we firmly hold with Scripture and the Lutheran Confessions that good works cannot lead to salvation; rather, salvation, won for us by Jesus Christ on the cross and given to us as a free gift, inevitably leads to good works. Having been saved, we now ask how we can live out that salvation in our daily working lives.

It has been said that there are really only three ethical philosophies. One is based on the ideas of Socrates and holds that knowledge and understanding are the only ultimate good and that there is no right or wrong except what the individual may determine within his or her own thinking. The second places value on the pursuit of power through strength—the survival of the fittest, with good being equated with dominance and victory. This is the thinking advocated by the nineteenth-century German philosopher Friedrich Wilhelm

[handwritten margin notes: 1. Knowledge (understanding) 2. Power 3. others]

Nietzsche. (Socrates, by the way, was forced to drink hemlock, and Nietzsche ended up in an insane asylum.) Finally, there is the teaching of Jesus, who calls on us to watch out for the interests of our fellow man as we follow the Golden Rule. It is this third viewpoint that will guide us as we look at the ethical problems encountered in the modern workplace.

This is not intended to be a theological exposition or academic treatise. It is intended to be a handbook for real people in real-life situations. It might further be used for adult Bible studies in the local congregation or as a textbook for classroom ethics study. We have provided case studies for discussion according to the ethical guidelines suggested here. So, as we launch into our discussion, let us look first at the biblical foundation that underlies the Christian's approach to ethics in the workplace.

Raymond L. Hilgert
Philip H. Lochhaas
James L. Truesdell

1
_____

A Biblical Overview of Christian Ethics

PHILIP H. LOCHHAAS

From my study window I saw him park his bright-yellow sports convertible and leap gracefully from it. What a handsome, confident young man! The thought crossed my mind, "Here is someone who has everything going for him!" I knew he had a high-paying position and a bright future in a growing high-tech industry. He didn't look at all like he sounded when he phoned for an appointment to see me. Sure enough, his confident stride was gone by the time he entered my study. He trudged through the door with his hands thrust deep in his jeans' pockets and his eyes fixed on the floor. I motioned him to a chair, but he remained on his feet, pacing back and forth.

At first he said nothing. Then haltingly he began, "I shouldn't ... have bothered you. There's probably ... nothing you can do to help me. No part of my world ...

even slightly resembles anything I was brought up to believe and expect." With that, a torrent of words began to pour out: "I don't know where to begin. Last week at work, with no help from anyone, I designed an improvement in our most popular product that will save thousands of dollars in manufacturing costs in addition to making the product more serviceable. But my supervisor presented my idea and drawings to our company CEO as entirely his own work. For that he received a special company commendation plus a sizeable bonus and a raise in pay. This is the man for whom I had 'covered' on numerous occasions, completing projects he'd bungled and solving problems that had left him completely baffled. I did these things so that his incompetence wouldn't lead to his dismissal. This is the thanks I get. I don't know what to do. I can't even talk comfortably with some of the men at work and certainly with none of the girls. It's like I'm from another planet. Their language ... their ridicule of values I have been taught ... the things they consider 'fun.' Pastor, do you have any idea what it's like 'out there'? Are there no longer any ethical principles? Any moral standards?"

"Yes," I assured him. "I know 'what it's like out there'!" Only the day before, a magazine had crossed my desk, *Smart Business for the New Economy*.[1] In very large print its cover called attention to the feature article, "The New Business Ethics: Cheating, Lying, Stealing—Technology Makes It Easy. Get Used to It." The author, John Galvin, in no way approved of these practices, but he warned that such is the ethics of the present and foreseeable future in business. "Be prepared!"

On another level, a skilled carpenter had told me a few days before, "My boss wanted me to build a staircase, but when I reported for the job, the materials supplied me were far below grade and I was to use nails where specifications have always called for screws. I held out my hands and told him that I was sure I couldn't make them do that kind of shoddy work. It's not the way I was brought up. 'Why,' I said, 'that stairway won't last 15 years.' He said that was okay—his warranty was only for 10 years. 'Now get busy if you want to keep your job!' What should I have done?"

Are there no ethics, no morals, to be found anywhere today? Yes, there are. You may rest assured that there are. From CEOs of multinational corporations to office workers, blue-collar men and women, and day laborers, there are thousands of moral, honorable, and yet successful men and women who maintain the highest moral and ethical standards. They would be uncomfortable if attention were called to their names because they take no credit for their exemplary conduct. As one CEO of a large corporation expressed it, "It is by the grace of God that I was raised with solid values in a Christian family, with mentors who knew right from wrong. I thank God daily for these and pray that I might by His grace continue in the things I was taught." He and many others resist the attempts of forces in society to modify their moral/ethical standards for the sake of expediency, monetary gain, popularity, or power.

Just what do these words *moral* and *ethical* mean? In view of today's conflicting and contradictory definitions of what is right and what is wrong, many people would be hard pressed to even define the words. In conversation, the two words are used as synonyms. They refer to either notions of right and wrong accepted by society or codes of conduct that have been established by an academic, governmental, or industrial entity. Questions still remain, however. What is the *source* of such formal "established" codes or "accepted" notions? By what standards is something deemed to be right, fair, and just?

ATTEMPTS AT EXPLAINING CONFLICTING MORAL/ETHICAL STANDARDS

The many conflicting and contradictory moral and ethical standards we encounter are explained by a simplistic statement that is frequently heard: "Well, it's because we live in a pluralistic society." By that is meant that there are so many different expressions of religion, race, ethnicity, and politics in our society that the individual may validly choose which moral/ethical standards he or she wishes to adopt. But *pluralistic* is a weak word; it only acknowledges a multiplicity of moral/ethical standards and does nothing to reconcile any to another.

The word of the moment is *multiculturalism*. It is a more specific word than *pluralism*, for it identifies the origins of various conflicting and contradictory moral/ethical standards. A multicultural society is one in which the preferences of many different cultures exist side by side as equal values in the present milieu. Multiculturalism per se raises no alarms for Christian people. On the contrary, it can be seen as quite a boon to society. Multiculturalism gives rise to a rich variety of traditions, languages, customs, foods, and styles of furniture and clothing.

Of great concern to the Christian, however, are the effects of *misdirected* multiculturalism on morals and ethics. For too many people, multiculturalism means that there can be no objective truth, no absolutes of right and wrong, and even no such thing as factual history. The concept of validating all human behavior under the protection of one's culture may spawn both tragic and comic situations. A person may attempt to justify openly carrying firearms in public as an expression of his or her "culture." Another, as part of his or her "culture," may disregard civil laws. May not similar applications be made to validate the Holocaust, genocide in Yugoslavia, and the genital mutilation of young girls in parts of Africa?

Trivialization of multiculturalism comes about when the word is applied to things that have no true cultural identity, such as "the culture of childhood," "the culture of pro-choice," and even "the culture of Microsoft"! Such application of multiculturalism to situations or conditions instead of true culture contributes to the establishment of conflicting and contradicting moral/ethical codes. Right and wrong are determined by circumstances that have no origin in culture.

A better name for the kind of misdirected multiculturalism that excuses and justifies everything is *nihilism*. Nihilism in the final analysis is deification of each individual human as the only significant reality. In a nihilistic society, moral/ethical choices are often governed by slogans, like "Each person must create his/her own happiness," "Do your own thing," "Immediate gratification is our one true heritage," "There are no absolutes," "You only go 'round once in life," and "Whatever ... I'm worth it!"

The results of such misdirected multiculturalism are ludicrous as well as tragic. A notorious pornographer becomes a cultural hero. An athlete known for his immoral life becomes a cultural icon. Movies and videos glorifying sexual immorality, violence, political chicanery, and crude behavior are to be considered valid cultural expressions. This worldview appears to be an attempt to put anyone's personal tastes or practices beyond criticism.

Many things are acceptable in the name of multiculturalism. You see the deletion of references to religious movements from history books, even though the understanding of a whole era may depend on them. Pictures of students wearing crosses are removed from school yearbooks because they offend multiculturalists. Distribution of Christian literature is banned on school campuses, while literature from atheist, gay-rights, and neopagan groups is permitted because these represent multiculturalism. It's okay to print newspaper cartoons lampooning Christianity but not ones denigrating Islam, Hinduism, Buddhism, and Judaism because these represent multiculturalism.

Even when dealing with genuine cultures, no success has been found in reconciling conflicting and contradictory moral/ethical standards. An oft-told tale describes an English officer's encounter with a pious Hindu during the time Great Britain exercised sovereignty over India. The Hindu gentleman confronted the officer with the challenge, "My culture and my conscience tell me that it is my right to throw a (living) widow on her husband's funeral pyre." The officer replied, "My culture and my conscience tell me to hang you if you do!" This is an extreme example, no doubt, but one that is repeated in subtler forms each day of our lives. Is stealing wrong? Ask the child who has been sent to the principal's office and placed on detention for stealing a pencil from her classmate; she will say, "Yes, what I did was wrong." Ask the entrepreneur who through industrial espionage has stolen a competitor's secrets; he may answer, "No, it's part of doing business. It's simply a risk in industry." Ask a man who has stolen in order to feed his starving family, and the answer you might receive is, "I had no other choice." And if the question "Is stealing wrong?" is put to you or me, we are expected to reply, "It all depends ..."

Both pluralism and multiculturalism may attempt to identify the roots of the contradictory moral/ethical standards our age embraces, but an attempt at explanation is not the same as reconciliation of conflicting beliefs. Therefore, a new buzzword is needed to address our moral/ethical inconsistencies. Now the word of the moment becomes *postmodern*. *Postmodern* is an oxymoron, to be sure, for how can anything be later than the latest? It is used, however, to denote an age in which truth, reality, and morals are at best only relative; they are no more or less than a person *perceives* them to be. Absolute standards in morals and ethics are rejected by postmodernism. No reconciliation of conflicting standards is needed! Each individual's choice must be considered as valid as the next person's.

Of course, the safeguard is always added that an individual's choice of lifestyle must not impinge upon or harm another person. In the postmodern world, something that was formerly considered morally or ethically "wrong" can become "right" simply by redefining it. For example, modern, effective means of birth control, including abortion, are seen by many as having removed the wrongness of sex outside of marriage or marital unfaithfulness. Under this reasoning, even deviant sex acts are approved. But other safeguards are added. Make sure that there is mutual consent, and be sure to practice safe sex! Some have gone so far as to justify illegal activities if the law has made no provision for prosecuting them—if there is "no controlling legal authority."

The belief system that attempts to guide humankind through the morass of conflicting moral/ethical standards in the postmodern world is secular humanism. Secular humanism is based on the belief that "man is at last becoming aware that he *alone* is responsible for the world of his dreams, that he has *within himself* the power for its achievement" (*Humanist Manifesto I*, emphasis added).[2] *Humanist Manifesto II* further declares:

> We affirm that moral values derive their source from human experience. Ethics is *autonomous* and *situational*, needing no theological or ideological sanction. Ethics stems from human need and interest. ... *Reason and intelligence* are the most effective instruments that humankind possesses. ... Critical intelligence, infused by a sense of human caring, is the best method that humanity has for resolving problems. ... We believe in maximum individual autonomy consonant with social responsibility.[3]

[handwritten note: – Scripture is out.]

Notables who signed these manifestos include Margaret Sanger, the eugenics proponent who founded Planned Parenthood, and her socialist disciple Roger Baldwin, founder of the ACLU, as well as many prominent educators. Secular humanism's efforts to offer hope to a world in moral/ethical crisis are offered sincerely. They are nevertheless woefully inadequate, for they are based on the assumption that a man-made denial of God's existence is suddenly going to be a productive social standard of behavior. All human history attests the fact that, *on their own*, human beings have not made any progress in establishing consistent and universally accepted moral/ethical standards. The fact that humankind in its natural state is controlled by forces of evil is neither a figment of the imagination nor some fanatical religious claim lacking in supporting documentation or evidence.

The Word of God, the Bible, clearly recognizes, "For from within, out of men's hearts, come evil thoughts, sexual immorality, theft, murder, adultery, greed, malice, deceit, lewdness, envy, slander, arrogance and folly. All these evils come from inside and make a man 'unclean'" (Mark 7:21–23). History leaves no doubt that human beings are creatures fallen from the state in which they were originally created by God. In spite of secular humanism's evolutionary claims, humankind *on its own* has not progressed one bit morally or ethically from the gray dawn of history. Consider these confessions published in the *Humanist* magazine:

> We shall find it no easy task to mold a natural ethic strong enough to maintain moral restraint and social order without the supernatural consolations, hopes and fears. There is no significant example in history, before our time, of a society successfully maintaining moral life without the aid of religion.[4]

> Julian Huxley ... [American Humanist Association] humanist of the year in 1962, "thought it possible to establish a moral system which would be purely scientific in inspiration and

which would be capable of uniting mankind." But the humanist movement that Huxley projected has made only limited progress toward such a morality ... and we are still far from united on a number of basic questions ... and there's little hope of uniting the movement, let alone the world unless we find a way to a fuller consensus.[5]

The failure of secular humanism to improve the morals and ethics of the present age comes as no surprise, for, in the end, the goal of secular humanism is nothing less than the deification of humankind. By divine inspiration, the prophet Ezekiel puts such presumption into its proper perspective: "This is what the Sovereign LORD says: 'In the pride of your heart you say, "I am a god; I sit on the throne of a god." ... But you are a man and not a god, though you think you are as wise as a god'" (28:2).

If ethics depend on human instincts, culture, tradition, intuition, logic, or evolution, humankind will continue to seek, but never find, a consistent, workable standard of morals/ethics that applies to all human society and exists for the benefit of all.

What can rescue our age from sinking ever deeper into the abyss of self-deification into which secular humanism is leading it? It is obvious, or should be obvious, that if there is to be one consistent standard of ethics/morals, it must have its source outside human origin.

25

ONE PERFECT CODE OF CONDUCT: GOD'S MORAL LAW

The Holy Bible reveals God's will for how His creatures are to live with Him and with each other here in this world. This is God the Creator's moral/ethical code. It has not been withdrawn, modified, or amended since it was first put into the heart of humankind or set down in writing. It is summarized in the words, "Love the Lord your God with all your heart and with all your soul and with all your mind" and "Love your neighbor as yourself" (Matthew 22:37, 39). This perfect moral/ethical code, explained further in the Ten Commandments, is repeated throughout the Bible along with additional instruction and application:

> I am the LORD your God. ... You shall have no other gods before Me. ... You shall not make for yourself an idol. ... You shall not misuse the name of the LORD your God. ... Remember the Sabbath day by keeping it holy. ... Honor your father and your mother. ...You shall not murder. ... You shall not commit adultery. ... You shall not steal. ... You shall not give false testimony against your neighbor. ... You shall not covet ... anything that belongs to your neighbor. (Exodus 20:1–17)

It is the Christian believers' commission, as those who are "called out" (the *ekkleesia*, the holy Christian church), to share with all people the truth of eternal salvation in Jesus Christ and the timeless peace, joy, and love that are found in God's Word alone.

GOD'S MORAL LAW IS FOR ALL PEOPLE

It should be obvious that there must be some universal moral/ethical standard by which all people of every age are to live, or utter chaos and anarchy will rule. Life on this planet becomes intolerable when "every way of man is right in his own eyes" (Proverbs 21:2 KJV).

unrestricted Authority,

God's moral Law is *absolute*. We live together on one earth. It "is the LORD's, and everything in it, the world, and all who live in it" (Psalm 24:1). His moral Law applies uniformly to all people in every circumstance. We too often try to "compartmentalize" our lives into separate segments: family, work, recreation, worship, and more. Some such compartmentalization of our time is necessary if we are to keep from neglecting our family, our work, or our worship. However, we sometimes try to apply different moral/ethical standards to each role we fill. That in itself is the source of much of our indecisiveness, frustration, and tension. Moreover, we further try to compartmentalize morals and ethics themselves into such things as medical ethics, political ethics, business ethics, and so forth, as if there are to be separate codes for the several roles. These terms may be properly used when speaking of various *applications* of God's moral Law to our lives, but they may not be used to describe different *standards*. Just the words "Christian ethics" are sufficient. There is one moral Law and it applies in all circumstances.

Pleading ignorance of God's moral Law does not relieve humankind from living responsibly according to it. God has placed in the heart of man a conscience. While the conscience in man has been severely impaired by the cumulative effects of humankind's self-serving rebellion against God's moral standards, it still stands as a measure of right and wrong. Human beings have tried to rationalize the conscience away, subject it to cultural scrutiny, and silence it by means of frantic pleasure-seeking, drugs, and strong drink. But, imperfect as it has become, the conscience still serves as a checkpoint of God's moral Law. St. Paul, under divine inspiration, writes that those who suppress the truth of God by their wickedness are "without excuse" (Romans 1:20). Even the Gentiles "show that the requirements of the law are written on their hearts, their consciences also bearing witness, and their thoughts now accusing, now even defending them" (Romans 2:15).

In the same vein as these passages, all Holy Scripture speaks of God's moral Law with reverence and respect. God's moral Law is "perfect, reviving the soul. ... The statutes of the LORD are trustworthy. ... The commands of the LORD are radiant ... sure and altogether righteous" (Psalm 19:7–9). St. Paul, having been shown how his disobedience to God's moral Law was leading him to destruction, calls the Law "holy, righteous and good" (Romans 7:12). The apostle James finds identification of the "moral filth and the evil that is so prevalent" (James 1:21) in the Law's clear definition of right

28

and wrong—and he calls God's moral Law "the perfect law" (1:25), the "royal law found in Scripture" (2:8). He adds, "the wisdom that comes from heaven [respect for God's moral Law] is first of all pure; then peace-loving, considerate, submissive [obedient], full of mercy and good fruit, impartial and sincere" (3:17).

It is the commandments of God's "royal" moral Law that the Holy Scriptures urge "to be upon your hearts. Impress them on your children. Talk about them when you sit at home and when you walk along the road" (Deuteronomy 6:6–7). A warning is given, as well: "Be careful that you do not forget the LORD your God, failing to observe His commands. ... If you ever forget the LORD your God and follow other gods and worship and bow down to them, ... you will surely be destroyed ... for not obeying the LORD your God" (Deuteronomy 8:11, 19–20).

THE BAD NEWS
(THERE'S GOOD NEWS STILL COMING!)

In view of the perfection and purity of God's royal Law and the imminent destruction of all who disobey it, how can the existence of evil be so universally present in the world? Evil reaches out to taint and render ineffective our best efforts to live by God's precepts.

The source of all evil is the devil, Satan, the Prince of Darkness, who from the time of his first attempt to dethrone God and replace Him with himself, has sought to twist all of God's creation from its created shape and purpose. His primary target, of course, is humankind, the crown of God's creation. That is why his first temptation for humans was distortion of God's commands by first questioning and then denying them (Genesis 3:1, 4). Satan comes to humankind today with exactly the same temptation—to imagine a better good than that which God has created, a better way than the way of God's moral Law. Satan is not a creator; he seizes upon the good that God created and attempts to deform it.

Consider the words that the Bible uses to describe evil or disobedience to God. The word *sin* is literally "missing the mark," the mark being the perfection of God's Law. *Trespass* implies "stepping over the line" drawn by God's Law. *Iniquity* is "unevenness," straying from the level course of God's Law.

Sin is disobedience. No matter how private we consider certain sins, they are always against God. Furthermore, disobedience to God's Law is always against fellow humans as well. There are those who would deny this and point to the private nature of the seven deadly sins: pride, anger, envy, greed, sloth, gluttony, and lust. These may seem to be non-injurious to fellow human beings, but to implement these "private" sins, we humans manipulate others, exercise power over them, and evade our responsibilities toward them. Private sins accumulate to create the whole climate of society.

Today we hear much pious twaddle about individual rights and private choices. They say "no guilt can be attached to acts committed between consenting adults." Mark 7:21–23 makes it clear that "from within, out of men's hearts, come evil thoughts, sexual immorality, theft, murder, adultery, greed, malice, deceit, lewdness, envy, slander, arrogance and folly. All these evils come from inside and make a man 'unclean.'" No one is exempt from this uncleanness. "There is no difference, for all have sinned and fall short of the glory of God" (Romans 3:22–23).

Disobedience to God's moral Law leads to judgment. Romans 1 contains a horrendous catalog of immoralities so prevalent in our age—from outright worship of idols and the grossest sexual sins to the more common and "acceptable" sins of deceit, gossip, disobedience to parents, and ruthlessness. God further decrees that those who do such things (or even tolerate such things being done) "deserve death" (verse 32). It seems this should settle the matter as far as the topic of morals and ethics is concerned. We are all under judgment. It would seem that no one can be saved. Humanly speaking, it is impossible. But with God, all things are possible.

NOW THE GOOD NEWS

"The Lord ... is patient with you, not wanting anyone to perish, but everyone to come to repentance" (2 Peter 3:9). "God so loved the world that He gave His one and only Son, that whoever believes in Him shall not perish but have eternal life. For God did not send His Son into the world to condemn the world, but to save the world through Him" (John 3:16–17). Note the active verbs in this announcement: "God so *loved* ... He *gave* His one and only Son ... whoever *believes* in Him *shall have* eternal life." An aged professor was fond of repeating, "Hug those verbs!" The central message of the Holy Scriptures is not condemnation of human creatures who have set aside God's moral Law and pursued their own ways. That we all have done. The Good News (Gospel) is that Jesus Christ, God's Son, left His heavenly throne and came to earth, into our human existence, to take upon Himself the guilt and punishment for all our sins of rebellion and disobedience against God's moral Law—by dying on a cross as humankind's substitute. His subsequent rising from the dead and ascension into heaven were His heavenly Father's assurance that Jesus' sacrifice on behalf of humankind was accepted.

By faith in His sacrifice on our behalf, our falling short of God's moral standards is forgiven and our daily rebellion and disobedience to His Law is stricken from God's record. The perfect righteousness of Jesus Christ, Son of God, "comes through faith in Jesus Christ to all who believe" (Romans 3:22). "There is now no condemnation for those who are in Christ Jesus" (Romans 8:1). "It is God who justifies" (Romans 8:33).

THE GREATER DIGNITY
OF THE MORAL LAW

It is God's gracious gift of eternal salvation to all who believe that elevates His moral Law to the highest level of respect. There is no way that forgiveness minimizes the importance of the moral Law, as some may be tempted to conclude. St. Paul anticipated such an unwarranted assumption on the part of some who heard his message regarding forgiveness. After reiterating that a person is justified by faith (Romans 3:22), he asks, "Do we, then, nullify the law by this faith? Not at all! Rather, we uphold the law" (Romans 3:31). Paul also rejects such an impious notion: "What shall we say, then? Shall we go on sinning so that grace can increase? By no means!" (Romans 6:1–2). Instead, Paul calls attention to a whole new imperative for obeying God's moral Law:

> Therefore, I urge you, brothers, in view of God's mercy, to offer your bodies as living sacrifices, holy and pleasing to God—this is your spiritual act of worship. Do not conform any longer to the pattern of this world, but be transformed by the renewing of your mind. Then you will be able to test and approve what God's will is—His good, pleasing and perfect will. (Romans 12:1–2)

Paul continues with a long list of ways in which God's moral Law should be implemented in the lives of God's people, concluding with the statement, "Do not be overcome by evil, but overcome evil with good" (Romans 12:21).

The sequence of thought in the above passage is of vital importance to the Christian's understanding of the role of God's moral Law in his or her life. Paul begins chapter 12 of Romans with the word "therefore." "Therefore" always points backward to what was said previously. In his first 11 chapters of Romans, St. Paul has trumpeted God's mercies in Jesus Christ to those who have failed to measure up to his moral Law:

> But now a righteousness from God, apart from the law, has been made known, to which the Law and the Prophets testify. This righteousness from God comes through faith in Jesus Christ to all who believe. There is no difference, for all have sinned and fall short of the glory of God, and are justified freely by His grace through the redemption that came by Jesus Christ. God presented Him as a sacrifice of atonement, through faith in His blood. (3:21–25)

> He [Christ] was delivered over to death for our sins and was raised to life for our justification. (4:25)

> God demonstrates His own love for us in this: While we were still sinners, Christ died for us. (5:8)

"Therefore," Paul exhorts, in view of these unmerited mercies of God, "do not conform any longer to the pattern of this world" (12:1, 2). Paul recognizes that this is no easy task. All of us face daily pressures to "conform." The moral/ethical choices we face each day are rarely simple.

Let's face it. We desperately desire to be accepted by our peers. We surely don't wish to be thought of as "wimps" or "nerds." We strive for the ideal appearance conjured up by media advertising, even if it takes artificial hair, eyelashes, nails, bosoms, and derrieres—not to mention face lifts and tummy tucks. Many of these things may be harmless and at times amusing. The grave danger comes when we "conform to the pattern of this world" by compromising what is right and wrong according to God's moral Law. We find "logical" reasons to disobey God and excuse ourselves by blaming others in order to escape responsibility for our actions. Daily we face the dilemma that haunted St. Paul: "When I want to do good, evil is right there with me. ... What a wretched man I am! Who will rescue me from this body of death?" (Romans 7:21, 24).

After exclaiming, "Thanks be to God—through Jesus Christ our Lord" (Romans 7:25), Paul reassures the Christian believers, "You, however, are controlled not by the sinful nature but by the Spirit, if the Spirit of God lives in you" (Romans 8:9). The "renewing of your mind" in Romans 12:2 is God's Holy Spirit at work in us through the Holy Scriptures and the sacraments of Holy Baptism and the Lord's Supper. God's Word thus awakens in the believers a responsive love described in the words of St. Peter: "You are a chosen people, a royal priesthood, a holy nation, a people belonging to God, that you may declare the praises of Him who called you out of darkness into His wonderful light" (1 Peter 2:9).

There is a special worth and dignity in God's moral Law in that, having been forgiven by God's grace in Jesus Christ, we are provided by the moral Law with an avenue by which we can know how to serve God in humble gratitude all the days of our lives.

In his "Preface to the Epistle to the Romans," Martin Luther has written powerfully and succinctly of the relationship between our faith and our lives in this present world:

> Faith ... is a divine work in us. It changes us and makes us to be born anew of God; it kills the old Adam [our natural state of sin and rebelliousness against God] and makes altogether different men in the heart and spirit and mind and powers, and it brings with it the Holy Ghost. O, it is a living, busy, active, mighty thing, this faith; and so it is impossible for it not to do good works incessantly.[6]

THE WORST OF TIMES AND THE BEST OF TIMES

We live in the worst of times. Immorality confronts us daily in the marketplace, the media, the neighborhood, and sometimes the family. Unethical practices abound in the workplace, where we spend a great deal of our time facing standards that are quite different from our own. There are two things to be considered in the workplace: relationships between supervisors and other employees, and relationships with the public and clients. These have been categorized as internal and external customers. The Bible is explicit in the standards to which the Christian is to adhere. It does not, however, spell out in detail the exact manner in which we are to deal with each specific problem we encounter. Instead, God has given us His Spirit in the Word and the Sacraments to help us use His gifts to make and implement decisions to His glory.

There are always difficult questions in these worst of times: How am I to handle immoral expectations on the part of my superiors or fellow workers? Must I close my eyes to impurity, cheating, theft? Is it unethical for me to not "blow the whistle" on others' unethical practices? Must I always defend an unfairly treated and unpopular co-worker and from that moment on be identified with him or her? Must I just quietly grin and bear it when I have been treated unjustly? Must I terminate my employment if it requires performing unethical deeds on behalf of my employer? Must I accept "everybody does it" and "it's part of doing business" as justification for immoral/unethical actions?

These are difficult choices—especially in view of the consequences that may follow. The following chapters will deal with sound principles upon which to make our decisions, as well as case histories for our consideration and discussion.

While we may live in the worst of times as far as the pressures of immorality upon us are concerned, these are the best of times for exemplifying God's moral/ethical standards in the marketplace. Our society does not even begin to comprehend how dependent it is on its Christian components for stability. Nothing would bring an end more quickly to every field of noble endeavor than the removal of Christian people who will not compromise moral/ethical integrity in order to gain power, wealth, or pleasure. Not only do those who seek to glorify God in their daily lives contribute to the common good of all, but they also bring hope to the timid, who may be like-minded and looking for supportive encouragement.

We may be living in the so-called postmodern age, but it is certainly not the post-Christian age, as some have maintained. The church may have less influence in society than in the Middle Ages, but it is still a powerful force for good. Each day is a day of opportunity to declare the grace of God in providing eternal life through His Son's death for the sins of the world. Never in the history of the world have there been such means to reach out to multitudes with the Word of God. Each day is a day of opportunity to draw from God's Word and Sacraments the Spirit's energy that will move us to glorify God in our daily pursuits. St. Paul wraps up the Christian's commission in these words to the Philippian believers:

Do everything without complaining or arguing,
so that you may become blameless and pure,
children of God without fault in a crooked and
depraved generation, in which you shine like
stars in the universe as you hold out the word
of life. (Philippians 2:14–16)

The Christian's response to the pluralistic, multi-cultural, postmodern society begins with knowing who he or she is. That may appear to be elementary, but we should be consciously aware that we are beings who live in a vertical relationship with God and a horizontal relationship with our fellow humans. Put these two directions together and they form a cross—and it is the cross of our Lord Jesus Christ that defines who we are. It is through the cross of our Lord Jesus Christ that we know our God as a heavenly Father whose love and protection are new to us every morning. It is through the cross of our Lord Jesus Christ that we bring hope to our world. It is through the cross of our Lord Jesus Christ and the forgiveness it brings that our interactions with our fellow humans are shaped, whether they are familial, social, recreational, environmental, or related to the workplace.

Facing daily attacks on God's moral/ethical standards can be a wearying experience. But, calling attention to the faith and assurance of the multitudes of faithful believers of whom "the world was not worthy" (Hebrews 11:38), the holy writer urges us:

Therefore, since we are surrounded by such a great cloud of witnesses, let us throw off everything that hinders and the sin that so easily entangles, and let us run with perseverance the race marked out for us. Let us fix our eyes on Jesus, the author and perfecter of our faith, who for the joy set before Him endured the cross, scorning its shame, and sat down at the right hand of the throne of God. Consider Him who endured such opposition from sinful men, so that you will not grow weary and lose heart. (Hebrews 12:1–3)

QUESTIONS FOR DISCUSSION

1. When, if ever, ought the church to modify its stance on contemporary moral issues in keeping with societal changes? Explain in light of 1 Samuel 15:29 and Malachi 3:6.

2. In former times some church bodies considered buying life insurance sinful. Other churches condemned dancing or card playing. Today, many Christians have changed their stance. Are they right to do so?

3. How do we rightly apply Scripture to moral issues?

4. This chapter affirms that "Jesus came into the world to negate our sin, not our humanity." What does that mean?

5. Christ shared our humanity (Hebrews 2:14). How can this truth help you in times of moral confusion and temptation (Hebrews 4:15–16).

6. How may self-imposed virtues contradict the grace of God? See Galatians 6:14.

7. Who or what are you most likely to blame when you give in to immoral/unethical pressures at work (yourself, a co-worker, the situation, the job itself)? How can we stop playing the "blame game"? See 1 John 1:5–10.

8. How can we stop the cycle of unethical practices in the workplace without appearing to sit in judgment on others?

9. Is the act of covering up evidence of someone else's wrongdoing as serious a sin as the initial unethical act? Why or why not? See Proverbs 11:20 and 12:17.

Consider the scenarios described below in light of the chapter you just read and the Scriptures cited in it. Remember who you are by God's grace in Christ—a new person, holy in God's sight. How does that baptismal identity shape your actions in each case here?

1. You are ordered to falsify an expense account.

2. A friend suggests you use your company's special purchasing discounts to buy personal items.

3. A supplier offers you "gifts" as an incentive to direct your company's purchases in her direction.

NOTES

1. John Galvin, "The New Business Ethics: Cheating, Lying, Stealing—Technology Makes It Easy. Get Used to It," *Smart Business for the New Economy* (June 2000): 86–97.

2. *Humanist Manifestos I* and *II* (Buffalo: Prometheus Books, 1977).

3. Ibid.

4. *Humanist* (February 1977): 26.

5. *Humanist* (March/April 1979): 41.

6. Martin Luther, "Preface to the Epistle to the Romans," *Works of Martin Luther* (Philadelphia: Muhlenberg Press, 1931), 451.

✦

Ethics in the Workplace— Perspectives from Philosophers and Practitioners

RAYMOND L. HILGERT

WHATEVER HAPPENED TO ETHICS?

In its May 25, 1987, issue, *Time* magazine devoted an entire cover page and feature section to several articles collectively entitled "Whatever Happened to Ethics?" The subtitle of this feature section asserted: "Assaulted by Sleaze, Scandals and Hypocrisy, America Searches for Its Bearings." Several articles highlighted wholesale revelations of unethical and illegal conduct as reported in the media concerning individuals in business, government, medicine, Law, and even the religious community. One article entitled "What's Wrong?" claimed that "hypocrisy, betrayal and greed unsettle the nation's soul." An article focusing upon American business practices stated, "Not since the reckless 1920s has the business world seen such searing scandals. White collar scams abound; insider trading; money laundering; greenmail. Greed combined with technology has made stealing more tempting than ever. Result: what began as the decade of the entrepreneur is becoming the age of the pin-striped outlaw." Although the tone of each of the *Time* articles was pessimistic, a concluding article also described how leaders throughout our country were becoming concerned about the need for reasserting ethical values and principles. In summarizing this hopeful attitude, *Time* said, "At a time of moral disarray, America seeks to rebuild a structure of values."[1]

CONTINUING EVIDENCE OF MORAL DECLINE

Unfortunately, however, there does not appear to have been significant change in the overall ethical climate in the ensuing years since the *Time* article. Especially in business and the workplace—and despite laudable efforts by some business leaders and others—unethical conduct and questionable behavior by employers and employees continue to be rampant throughout all segments of the workplace. For example, a major survey in 1999 revealed that about three out of four responding employees reported witnessing some form of unethical conduct during the previous year, but most employees acknowledged that they did nothing or very little about it. Employees explained that they often were inclined to look the other way because they felt it would not be worth their time to report ethical infractions. They believed that they might be retaliated against for reporting unethical behavior of supervisors, managers, and fellow employees. About two-thirds of the reported unethical behavior was attributed to pressures on supervisors and employees to meet schedules or to meet unrealistic earnings goals. Unethical practices and behavior included deception, false or misleading promises to customers and suppliers, various forms of discrimination, falsification of financial data, and stealing or embezzling. A majority of the companies whose personnel were surveyed had published codes of ethics and had held training programs in ethics, but respondents considered these to be mostly "window dressing" and not credible.[2]

A recent problem is that of e-mail abuse. In another 1999 large-scale survey, some 90 percent of the workers admitted that they used their company's Web-linked computers at work without authorization, and many of them admitted to spending considerable amounts of time each day on the Web or sending personal messages from company computers, conducting personal business, playing games, and other forms of unauthorized activities. Only about one in ten of the respondents said that Web surfing and computer use for nonwork reasons was unethical, and they avoided doing this on their employers' premises.[3]

If these statistics are even partially accurate, they suggest that many Christians must be included within the moral decline and ethical lapses in business and the workplace. Have Christians, too, become so secular in their day-to-day work lives that they do not really practice what they know to be the teachings of Scripture? Do they ignore their responsibility to act as Christians in the workplace?

Many observers attribute the decline in ethical standards in the workplace to the age-old sin of greed. A *U.S. News and World Report* article, entitled "The State of Greed," claimed that the problem of greed was apparent and rising among all classes and was strongly linked to many of the country's social problems. This article suggested that greed was thriving for three major reasons, namely: (1) Our economic and social structure encourages many more people to pursue and attain wealth; (2) Huge numbers of middle-class individuals have become part of the quest for wealth, as they continue to invest in securities and mutual funds and expand the use of credit cards; and (3) The desire for wealth has overpowered other values, like respect for others, honesty at work, and participation in the community. As examples, the article reported that $435 billion is stolen from U.S. employers annually by their employees—some 6 percent of an average firm's revenues and three times more than in 1960. Twenty-five percent of Americans admit to some form of tax cheating, which amounts to $100 billion annually; fraud in workers compensation programs is estimated at $5 billion or more each year. Summarizing the aggregate situation, *U.S. News and World Report* stated: "It's not the desire to make money that corrodes souls. It's desire for money that overwhelms every other consideration."[4] This is nothing new. Centuries ago St. Paul wrote, "The love of money is a root of all kinds of evil" (1 Timothy 6:10).

THE IMPORTANCE OF ETHICAL BEHAVIOR TO OUR ECONOMIC SYSTEM

It would be easy for Christians to be pessimistic and complacent about the secular world. This is often the case in the business and work environment, where Christians lose sight of the importance of ethical choices not only to their personal lives, but also to the entire functioning of our free enterprise, market-based competitive system and our democratic way of life.

A primary reason why high ethical standards and behavior are so important is that our economic system fundamentally is based upon decisions that are made by individuals and organizations. Ben Franklin, one of our country's great founders, once said that democracy was dependent upon having a "virtuous people." Similarly, it could be argued that a free-enterprise system depends upon people who behave ethically throughout the workplace environment. For example, decisions of managers in most businesses involve a myriad of seemingly conflicting claims and interests. Business managers must decide in ways that will bring profits or advantages to owners and stockholders. At the same time, however, a business firm is expected to provide customers with a product or service that is of high quality and available at a reasonable or fair price. Employees must be paid competitive wages and benefits and provided some security if good employees are to be attracted and retained. The business must meet its obligations to creditors, suppliers, and others and also its obligations to satisfy requirements of government and promote the general welfare. These typically involve difficult considerations pertaining to laws, taxes, environmental issues, and the quality of community life.

In essence, our free-enterprise economic system is largely based upon trust among numerous parties that all will act toward some form of mutual satisfaction or mutual gain. Our system and democratic way of life are based upon a premise that benefits from decisions and transactions should not go solely to one person or one group, because there are numerous other individuals and groups whose own self-interests should be considered. Certainly, every Christian should recognize that business and workplace decisions that ignore the interests of others are hardly in keeping with biblical teachings.

Sadly, a widespread lack of trust seems to dominate the American workplace environment. A 1999 study of about 7,500 employees found that only about half of the respondents trusted their companies and managers to be fair and honest with them. Elements that diluted employee trust were listed: managers not respecting others, not sharing information, giving unwarranted negative feedback, gossiping and backbiting, being inconsistent, and not involving others in workplace decisions. Interestingly, this same study indicated that companies where the majority of employees said that they did trust their top managers had shareholder returns that were 40 percent higher than those companies where distrust was dominant.[5]

REASONS FOR UNETHICAL CHOICES IN BUSINESS AND THE WORKPLACE

Why do managers, supervisors, employees, and others—Christians and non-Christians alike—often make unethical decisions, or choices that do not adequately recognize or balance the interests of others and fairly meet other obligations? For many people, greed and a desire for personal gain are often the paramount reasons for their actions. Some individuals do not really recognize or observe moral or ethical principles in business, or they conveniently ignore them as not being a required component of their firm's objectives. For some, the terms "business ethics" and "workplace ethics" are oxymorons, that is, contradictions in meaning, because ethics does not fit in a competitive world where people are pursuing their own personal gain and self-interest.

Many people seek to attain a short-term maximum advantage. They do not see beyond the immediate deal or decision, and they do not care that a good reputation may be crucial to long-term success. Some people do not make good ethical choices because they are weak or ignorant about what to do. These individuals may close their eyes to ethical misconduct because they fear retribution if they should report it. Perhaps they don't want to be labeled a "do-gooder" or "squealer." Many individuals find it difficult to decide what to do in situations posing conflicts among their various self-interests. When they belong to different groups within a conflict, they are unable or unwilling to apply ethical principles to their decision making. These people try to muddle their way through conflicting situations they encounter without having any coherent moral/ethical framework to guide their choices.

One reason there has been so much evidence of ethical misconduct in business is that too many managers, employees, and leaders—of whom Christians certainly are a segment—have not clearly specified and insisted upon high ethical standards in their organizations. People frequently take their cues from their leadership. If leaders are not setting the example, many people become indifferent. Too often, Christian leaders do not reflect the standards that would be expected of them. Followers who try to shift the blame to a leader or someone else cannot claim a sound ethical foundation. Ethical choices ultimately are an individual matter; we are accountable for the choices we make.

Ethics: The Study of the Ideal Human Character

The term *ethics* is often interpreted as being a fuzzy concept that has something to do with human attitudes and behavior. Ethics may be viewed as being very subjective and relative to each situation, sort of a "play dough" that people can manipulate to their own preference. Such a view is quite limited and far from the truth.

Ethics concern judgments about what is right and wrong and conclusions about what ought to be instead of what is. There are two general types of ethical emphasis: (1) *descriptive*, in which are provided pronouncements and analyses of moral judgments as related to formulations from great religious and philosophical writings, and (2) *normative*, in which prescriptions are given concerning what is right and wrong, along with admonitions to do right.

Throughout history, religious and moral philosophers have debated questions about morality, values, right and wrong, and the like. We now turn to the major schools of thought. These can be helpful in understanding some of the pronouncements that have been suggested, which Christians, too, can utilize when confronted with difficult choices.

SCHOOLS OF PHILOSOPHICAL STUDY IN ETHICS[6]

There certainly are areas of overlap in various ethical schools of thought, and people—both Christians and non-Christians—will differ over some of these concepts. Nevertheless, they do suggest how philosophers have tried to grapple with ethical and moral principles in their descriptions and prescriptions for the ideal human character.

Utilitarianism is the name given to the philosophical school that stresses that one should behave in such a manner that one's actions will realize the greatest good for the greatest number of people. The greatest good can be measured in benefits or harms that can result from the way someone decides or behaves. Some people associate this with the Golden Rule stated by Christ in His Sermon on the Mount (Matthew 7:12). The Golden Rule, which is found in various forms in a number of religious traditions throughout the world, advocates treating other people in the same manner as one would wish to be treated. This principle requires an individual to place himself in the other person's shoes to do what is best.

Rights and Duties ethical proponents, often identified with the renowned German philosopher Immanuel Kant, emphasize that every person has basic rights in a moral universe. Every society has laws that citizens are expected to follow, such as acting with honesty, honoring contracts, keeping promises, and the like. These help people relate to each other in ways that enable the society to exist. Kant claimed that one of the most basic human rights is the right to be treated with respect. This imposes on everyone a duty to treat others with respect. He argued that human morality is possible only if people have free will to choose and if they believe in the real existence of God and an immortal soul.

Enlightened Self-interest philosophers emphasize that decisions made by individuals to benefit themselves can be morally and ethically proper if one adequately considers and weighs the harms, benefits, and rights of others first. People make choices in business and in the workplace in their own self-interest. These can be ethical if they do not arbitrarily hurt others and if they minimize the harms and damages to the rights of others. A market-based capitalistic system, as expounded upon by the eighteenth-century Scottish economist and philosopher Adam Smith, argues that individuals acting in their own self-interest without seeking to destroy or harm the interests of others will bring about the greatest good for the greatest number of people, especially in the long term. This is consistent with the utilitarian viewpoint mentioned previously.

Distributive Justice is the term for the emphasis on justice and fairness as requisites for making ethical decisions. In business applications, it is impossible or impractical in numerous decisions to distribute all benefits and burdens on a totally equal basis. Here the concepts of justice and fairness require that inequalities in distribution of benefits and harms must come from "ethically acceptable methods" in creating those differences. For example, differences in wages and salaries should be based upon actual and recognized differences in responsibilities, training, and position; differences created arbitrarily by race, gender, and other irrelevant distinctions would be unjust.

Moral Life schools include the writings of both religious and secular philosophers who recognize that religious teachings serve as the foundation for human morality and ethics. These emphasize that there is a moral force in the universe (e.g., God) that gives guidance to human beings concerning what is right and wrong. Ancient Greek philosophers upheld virtues that were expected by their gods. The moral life is part of the Christian's faith in Christ for salvation, and it is Scripture that expects believers to pursue virtues and to avoid vices. These principles, as noted by Dr. Lochhaas, are embodied in the Ten Commandments and the Sermon on the Mount. St. Paul further identified the three major Christian virtues as being faith, hope, and love. The Bible is replete with examples of how Christians are to apply them. Of course, no Christian can earn salvation just by living a moral life. Rather, a moral life gives evidence of salvation.

A MODEL OF ETHICAL LEVELS FOR UNDERSTANDING WORKPLACE DECISION MAKING

The philosophical schools or areas of emphasis for ethical study described above apply to all aspects of human behavior. In order to focus more narrrowly, many firms and institutions in business, government, and professional fields have developed their own ethical codes. [7]

Business and workplace decision making has been the subject of much ethical debate and controversy. In order to better understand the range of alternatives and their applications in business and organizational settings, we will consider a number of levels of ethical decision making and conduct.

Figure 2–1 (page 56) was developed by two professors at the Olin School of Business of Washington University in St. Louis, Dr. Joseph W. Towle and myself. It does not comprehend all levels of conduct, but the model does depict a range of possible areas of choice. The model shows these ethical levels as following an upward path leading to the Judeo-Christian ethic as the ultimate guide for workplace behavior.

Some people do not even regard applicable laws and regulations as being restraints upon their actions, much less ethical obligations. This level can be referred to as the Illicit or Illegal ethic. Most people, of course, view this level as being unacceptable and quite unethical. However, for a small minority, "anything goes." They will violate laws in order to attain their objectives. In the business world, greed has no boundaries in the eyes of some people, as they disregard the law in order to achieve profits, cheat someone else, or attempt to extort some other form of personal gain. Sadly, this has resulted in well-publicized arrests, charges, and convictions throughout the business community, as certain individuals ignored the law and violated positions of trust in order to achieve personal wealth.

Second is the Legal or Compliance ethic, which some people consider to be the only required ethical

ETHICAL LEVELS*

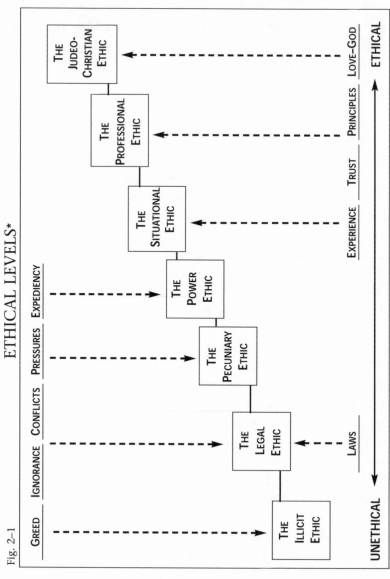

Fig. 2–1

*Developed by Dr. Joseph W. Towle and Dr. Raymond L. Hilgert, both of Washington University, St. Louis, Missouri.

standard in business decisions. These individuals reason that, as long as something is not prohibited by law or regulations, it is acceptable, regardless of the consequences to others. Their primary ethical sources are the attorneys who provide the legal guidance and authority for their own and their firms' decisions and actions.

The next level, very similar to the Legal/Compliance ethical level, is the Pecuniary or Total Self-interest ethic. A person who operates by this standard thinks that it is appropriate to do whatever is necessary, to push the law to its outer limits, in order to take advantage of every loophole and weakness so as to maximize his personal gain. This type of ethic is almost totally self-serving. Although he operates just within the law, he shows little concern for the rights of others. "Achieve the most for myself" is his code. He will run roughshod over others.

Close to this is what is described as the Power ethic, which is based primarily upon power relationships between individuals and groups. The Power ethic, one often justified by a market-based competitive framework, assumes an adversarial stance, group against group, individual against individual. Extreme competitiveness, exploitation of weakness, domination of the other party, and heedlessness of the consequences to the other side when taking advantages are manifestations of the Power ethic. An example of the Power ethic for many decades has been the American labor relations system, particularly in the bargaining tactics used by both unions and management. The adversarial posture between management and employees continues to dominate employment relationships in many firms, leading to behavior in which both sides utilize power tactics in order to attain the upper hand against each other.

The next level has been described as the Situational or Contingency ethic. The Situational ethic does not necessarily reject moral or ethical standards, but it suggests that right and wrong largely reside in the eye of the beholder and that the end justifies the means. In business and workplace decisions, relativism and contingency to the situation are used to rationalize behavior that may be for the benefit of others or may become primarily self-serving. Situational ethics can be easily manipulated to justify actions that may be inconsistent, confusing, and harmful to others.

Much higher ethical standards are found in the Professional ethic, particularly as this stems from moral principles and values described by both secular and religious authorities. The Professional ethic includes written codes, standards, and principles as adopted and practiced by individuals, companies, organizations, professions, and occupational groups. It recognizes multiple relationships of human interdependency and responsibilities. The rights and claims of others must be observed, as well as the individual's own objectives and those of his or her organization.[7]

The highest standards are derived from the

Judeo-Christian ethic, which is concerned with one's ultimate relationships both to God and to fellow human beings. It is built upon the Old and New Testaments, which emphasize responsibilities, love, and concern for others as moral duties. The Judeo-Christian ethic expects workplace behavior that is compatible with the needs of individuals and society. For the Christian, this certainly should be the highest and most-desired ethical level. Indeed, it is not optional, since it contains guiding principles for living the total Christian life. We are to exemplify Christlike behavior as God gives us grace and strengthens our faith through Word and Sacraments. This is the standard St. Paul exhorted Christians to follow in living as "new creatures" and "ambassadors for Christ" (2 Corinthians 5:17–21).

[handwritten margin note: Note: The purpose is for the sake of showing people the mind/heart of Christ not to earn salvation]

WORKPLACE DECISIONS MAY BE ETHICALLY CONFLICTING

Although the model described here can be helpful in guiding one's ethical choices and behavior, realities of business and workplace objectives and pressures can be confusing and conflicting, even to the most dedicated of Christians. Shifting priorities, conflicts between profit/wage/customer objectives, directives posed by unethical bosses, and numerous other dilemmas often place individuals in tenuous circumstances where their ethical and religious values are challenged. Unfortunately, some Christians rationalize their predicaments by asserting that it is not possible for them always to behave ethically in their work situations. Nevertheless, the Christian in the workplace usually has a range of options. In the next chapter, we will discuss practical approaches for making ethical decisions that can be consistent with the Judeo/Christian level of ethical behavior and the Christian's desire to manifest a moral life according to it.

QUESTIONS FOR DISCUSSION

1. Give some examples of who people might believe that America is in a state of "moral disarray" How might we explain the reasons why?

2. Give examples of moral decline and misconduct that have been prominently reported in recent years. How does this compare with Bible times? See Genesis 6:5–8; 18:20–21. Why might the media tend to over-report the negative and under-report the positive aspects of our society?

3. How are government, business, and the economy ultimately faith issues? See Luke 14:25–33; Matthew 22:17–21. Why are ethical behavior and trust important for our economic system? Do you think there has been a decline of trust within the workplace and throughout our country's business, political, and social institutions?

4. Identify and discuss reasons why many individuals, including Christians, frequently make unethical choices in business and the workplace. See 1 Corinthians 6:7–11; Romans 7:14–25a. What hope do we gain from the last verse of each of these texts?

5. Part of the dictionary definition of ethics is its reference to the study of the "ideal human character." Why is this concept the cause for so many struggles? Will we/can we ever reach the status of that "ideal human character" in this life? What is our hope as believers? See Ephesians 2:8–10.

6. Identify and discuss each of the following schools of philosophical study in ethics:

   a. Utilitarianism

   b. Rights and Duties

   c. Enlightened Self-interest

   d. Distributive Justice

   e. Moral Life

   Which of these is the most compelling to you? Why?

7. Why should a "moral life" still be a Christian's goal for living, even though no one can earn salvation just by living the moral/ethical life? See James 2:14–17.

8. Review the model of ethical levels for understanding business/workplace decision making. Try to identify examples of each of these levels that you have either experienced or are familiar with. Why does the Situational/Contingency level appeal to many individuals who face difficult choices? What does God promise as we make choices? See Jeremiah 29:11; Hebrews 13:5; Romans 8:28.

9. Refer to the Corporate Statements of Philosophy p 75 and Codes of Conduct included in the appendix to this chapter. Some critics interpret these as public

relations documents. Why might employees have a double standard, appearing to treat their firms' ethical policies as window dressing that does not need to be lived out? Can these types of ethical/value statements serve a useful purpose? How does Jesus uphold the "corporate policy" while holding people to a higher standard? See Matthew 5:17–32.

10. What business/workplace decisions present the most difficult moral and ethical dilemmas for committed Christians? What does Jesus remind the people in Matthew 16:24–26.

CASE PROBLEMS

These case problems are based on classroom papers by students at the Olin School of Business of Washington University. (Names in the case problems are fictional.)

"The Downsizing Dilemma," Nancy Wolfe

"Failed Training," Mark A. Dinman

"The Trip Expense Report," Scott Fields

◗ *The Downsizing Dilemma*

Principal Characters:

Jim Darst, manager, Accounting Consolidations and Reporting

Sara McCall, general ledger accountant

Cathy Banks, general ledger accountant

Robert Stern, director, Corporate Accounting

THE SITUATION

Jim Darst had been a supervisor in the corporate accounting department of a large manufacturing firm for over 15 years; currently he held the title of manager of the Department of Accounting Consolidations and Reporting. He was known as a "people manager" who excelled at promoting and developing top talent. Individuals in the firm enjoyed working for Jim owing to his expertise in the firm and his managerial skills.

His firm, however, was experiencing strong pressures to control its high administrative costs. The consolidations group had spent a great deal of money to automate and streamline its processes through systems upgrades and customization. Owing to current cost constraints, Jim had been told by his director, Robert Stern, to eliminate one of his general ledger accountant positions. The remaining position would be upgraded to reflect more accountability in the monthly consolidations workflow, as well as the increased workload.

Jim Darst had two general ledger accountants reporting to him. Cathy Banks had been with the firm for almost 20 years. Cathy did not have a college degree, but she had held several jobs within the corporate accounting function. Cathy had been a general ledger accountant for the past 10 years, and Jim viewed Cathy as his right arm. Cathy trained all new hires on the general ledger system. She was thorough, conscientious, and reliable. Overall, Jim evaluated Cathy as being an excellent employee.

Sara McCall, a fairly recent college graduate, had a bachelor's degree in accounting and computer systems applications. She had been working for the firm for about a year. Jim viewed Sara's performance as satisfactory and felt that she was progressing reasonably well and expanding upon her day-to-day responsibilities. Sara had previously suggested to Jim that ultimately she would like to transfer into another accounting or finance function in the firm (a common practice). Sara believed at this time, however, that it was in her best interests to stay in the consolidations group for at least another year to learn the ropes.

The week after Jim was told he must eliminate one of the general ledger accountant positions, Sara McCall came to Jim and told him she had been diagnosed with breast cancer. While the cancer had been caught in its early stages, she said she would need to miss a great deal of work owing to doctor appointments, chemotherapy, and radiation treatments. Sara wanted to continue to work, both at the office and from home. Jim responded that he had an enormous amount of respect for Sara and her ability to hold her head high.

Jim Darst was very torn about terminating one of his general ledger accountants. He had no real qualms about the performance of either individual. Jim's director, however, felt differently. Since the position was to be upgraded, Robert Stern believed the position should be filled by an individual with a four-year college degree and proficiency in computer technology and applications. Although Jim partially shared this sentiment, he believed that Cathy Banks was capable of handling increased responsibility. At the same time, Jim was concerned about Sara McCall. Would her health limit her ability to get insurance for a preexisting condition if she had to get a new job? Would she be able to handle the increased responsibility? The consolidations group had a strict timeline for closing the books and producing monthly financial statements. Would the department be able to rely on Sara in crunch times? Since the entire company was downsizing by cutting heads, there was no room for employee transfers. Jim also was concerned about any legal implications his decisions might have under federal laws that prohibit age and disability discrimination.

QUESTIONS FOR CASE PROBLEM

1. Identify the primary ethical issues in this situation.

2. (a) Define alternatives that are open to Jim Darst. (b) Evaluate the ethics of each of these alternatives by using the philosophical concepts and/or the model of ethical levels presented in this chapter.

3. If you were Jim Darst, what would you do, and why?

4. What might Jesus do in this situation? What has Jesus already done for us to accept us when we fail? See Luke 19:10.

▶ *Failed Training*

Principal Characters:

Jeanne Duffy, manager, Information Systems (I.S.),
    in a large retailing firm

John Sutton, computer operator and I.S. trainee report-
    ing to Jeanne Duffy

Bill Ryan, supervisor, computer department, and Sut-
    ton's previous supervisor

THE SITUATION

Jeanne Duffy had scheduled a luncheon appointment to meet with her newest department member,
John Sutton. John had just recently returned from a corporate technical training program six weeks early, having been unable to complete the required assignments
successfully. Looming in Jeanne's mind were the alternatives for action that she would have to choose from,
including possible termination of John's employment.
Jeanne had been I.S. manager for only two years, and
she had not had any prior experience with disciplining
or firing an employee. However, before she could come
to any conclusions, she needed more information, first
from John Sutton himself.

John, an African-American, had been employed by
the firm for about three years. His experience prior to
entering the Information Systems training program had
been in the computer operations area. Entering the I.S.
training program was a significant step in John's career,
because his goals included following a programming

career path. For John, it meant not only more and better job opportunities but also significantly more compensation. He had transferred to Jeanne's department just a few weeks prior to leaving for the 12-week class. As a result, Jeanne knew very little about John other than what she had acquired in a conversation with John's previous supervisor, Bill Ryan, who had approved both the internal transfer and the sending of John to the I.S. training program.

During lunch, it became very apparent to Jeanne that John now felt as though he was considered to be a failure. He was embarrassed personally and professionally by having to leave the training program early. In their conversation, John stressed that he really wanted another chance. When Jeanne asked him why he was unable to perform the training assignments adequately, John said that he had a medical condition that made him very tired, and he was unable to stay awake during the class sessions. This medical condition was surprising news to Jeanne. She wondered why John did not reveal this to her before he left for training. If he had done so, he could have stayed in his former position until he received the proper treatment and then gone to a later training class.

John Sutton then commented that he was not given the same attention and treatment in the training class as other students. When Jeanne probed further, John asserted that the lack of fair treatment was based on his race. Jeanne told John she would look into his complaints about the unfair treatment as well as the implications of his medical condition. She also gave him a form to take to his doctor that inquired whether or not John needed special consideration and what restrictions, if any, should be placed on John's ability to perform in his job as a programmer trainee. In the meantime, Jeanne told John to go home and get some rest for a couple of days while she investigated these matters.

After talking to the manager responsible for John's training class, it seemed evident to Jeanne that John had been treated fairly in all respects. In fact, the class manager said John was offered and given additional help on all the assignments with which he struggled. John had informed the class manager of having a problem staying awake in class, but John had not mentioned that he had a medical condition.

In a subsequent conversation with Bill Ryan (John's former boss), Bill told Jeanne that he was unaware of any medical condition such as John had described to Jeanne. In her conversation with Bill, Jeanne learned that Bill had placed John on a "performance improvement plan" during the past six months because of what Bill considered to be John's very poor attendance and work performance. This plan included a specific warning that unless John improved his attendance and the quantity and quality of his work, his employment would be terminated. This, too, was surprising news to Jeanne. She wondered why Bill would send a poorly performing employee to a rigorous training program. Jeanne suspected that Bill essentially had passed on his problem employee, John, to her department.

Jeanne Duffy was very troubled by all of this. She had to decide soon what to do, and she contemplated meeting with the firm's director of human resources for advice.

QUESTIONS FOR CASE PROBLEM

1. Identify the primary ethical issues in this situation.

2. (a) Define alternatives that are open to Jeanne Duffy. (b) Evaluate the ethics of each of these alternatives by using the philosophical concepts and/or the model of ethical levels presented in this chapter.

3. If you were Jeanne Duffy, what would you do, and why?

4. How do God's words in James 2:1–11 deal with prejudice? How does God's grace change our perspective for other believers—and non-believers as well? See Galatians 3:26–29.

▶ *Trip Expense Report*

Principal Characters:

Eddie Weber, engineer, Deltasonics Corporation, a large manufacturing firm in Midwest City

Bart Gompers, senior engineer, Deltasonics Corp.

Fred Barrett, technical manager, Moore Products, Inc., a large aluminum supplier

THE SITUATION

Fred Barrett had come to Midwest City to discuss several technical issues with Eddie Weber and Bart Gompers regarding a cooperative test program that both of their companies were engaged in. This test program was initiated to assess the structural performance of a relatively new aluminum plate product that Fred's company sold to Eddie and Bart's firm. Unknown to Eddie and Bart, Fred's company (Moore Products) was engaged in secret negotiations with Eddie and Bart's company (Deltasonics) to enter into a long-term agreement to provide huge quantities of this and other aluminum plate products. Fred offered to take Eddie and Bart out to dinner at a nearby fancy restaurant in order to continue their discussions.

While Fred was in the restroom, Eddie and Bart discussed whether or not their company's policy permitted them to allow Fred to pick up the check. (Fred had implied that he would.) They decided it was okay for them to accept, since they were not directly involved in aluminum plate purchasing decisions. After dinner, the check arrived and Fred Barrett proceeded to pay it. Eddie and Bart were relieved, since the bill was quite large. Further, since they were not on a business trip, they would have had to pay their share of the drinks and dinner from their own pockets.

About one month later, Eddie and Bart went on a business trip to West Coast City for an all-day meeting with Fred Barrett to discuss additional technical issues that had arisen. At the end of the day, Fred offered to take Eddie and Bart out to dinner, and Fred again indicated that he would pick up the tab. They went to a nice restaurant and continued to discuss business among other things, and Fred picked up the check. Afterward, when taking a taxi back to their hotel, Eddie and Bart noticed that a major motion picture was playing at a theater across the street from their hotel. They decided to go and see the movie.

The following week, Eddie and Bart were back in Midwest City filling out their expense reports for the trip they had just returned from. Bart stopped by Eddie's desk to drop off a copy of his completed report and discuss it with Eddie. Bart said he wanted to make sure that Eddie's meal expenses for the day Fred took them out to dinner were in line with Bart's. Bart had claimed $39 in meals for that particular day. However, Eddie knew that Bart had spent only about $5 that day on breakfast and that Fred had provided them with sandwiches during their working lunch. Rather than confront Bart about the $39, Eddie responded that he had spent $4 that day on breakfast.

In their conversation, Bart began complaining about how it was not fair that the employees of some of their main customers (including the U.S. government) got a fixed per diem payment for travel and meal expenses, and employees could keep whatever they didn't spend. Deltasonics Corporation only reimbursed based on actual expenditures. Bart also reminded Eddie that they had paid to see a movie for which they could not be reimbursed since there was no line on the company's reimbursement form for this. Bart explained to Eddie that their boss routinely padded his meal expenses to cover various forms of entertainment that were not reimbursable, up to the daily allowable meal limit of $45. Bart argued that the two of them probably would have spent more than $35 each if they had had to pay for their own meals, and the company would have had to reimburse them accordingly. Bart ended the conversation by saying he really, really hoped that Eddie's expense report was similar to his.

After Bart Gompers left, Eddie Weber was not sure what to do. Eddie and Bart's boss was the one who had to approve their expense report, and he was known to sign them without much thought other than to make sure no limits were exceeded and that no nonreimbursable items were listed. Although Bart was not Eddie's supervisor, Eddie knew that Bart had a large say in Eddie's performance review, which was coming next month. Also, Eddie had always gotten along very well with Bart, and they were good friends.

QUESTIONS FOR CASE PROBLEM

1. Identify the primary ethical issues in this situation.
2. (a) Define alternatives that are open to Eddie Weber. (b) Evaluate the ethics of each of these alternatives by using the philosophical concepts and/or the model of ethical levels presented in this chapter.

3. If you were Eddie Weber, what would you do, and why?

4. How does Matthew 5:13–16 remind us of the way Christ's light might guide our lives?

CORPORATE STATEMENTS OF PHILOSOPHY AND CODES OF CONDUCT

✦

THE BOEING COMPANY

OUR VALUES

In all our relationships we will demonstrate our steadfast commitment to:

LEADERSHIP

We will be a world-class leader in every aspect of our business—in developing our team leadership skills at every level; in our management performance; in the way we design, build and support our products; and in our financial results.

INTEGRITY

We will always take the high road by practicing the highest ethical standards, and by honoring our commitments. We will take personal responsibility for our actions, and treat everyone fairly and with trust and respect.

QUALITY

We will strive for continuous quality improvement in all that we do, so that we will rank among the world's premier industrial firms in customer, employee, and community satisfaction.

CUSTOMER SATISFACTION

Satisfied customers are essential to our success. We will achieve total customer satisfaction by understanding what the customer wants and delivering it flawlessly.

PEOPLE WORKING TOGETHER

We recognize our strength and our competitive advantage is—and always will be—people. We will continually dream and share ideas and knowledge. We will encourage cooperative efforts at every level and across all activities in our company.

A DIVERSE AND INVOLVED TEAM

We value the skills, strengths, and perspectives of our diverse team. We will foster a participatory workplace that enables people to get involved in making decisions about their work that advance our common business objectives.

GOOD CORPORATE CITIZENSHIP

We will provide a safe workplace and protect the environment. We will promote the health and well-being of Boeing people and their families. We will work with our communities by volunteering and financially supporting education and other worthy causes.

ENHANCING SHAREHOLDER VALUE

Our business must produce a profit, and we must generate superior returns on the assets entrusted to us by our shareholders. We will ensure our success by satisfying our customers and increasing shareholder value.

✦

HERSHEY FOODS CORPORATION

STATEMENT OF CORPORATE PHILOSOPHY

As a major diversified company, we are in business to make a reasonable profit and adequate return on our investment and to enhance the value of our shareholders' investment.

We recognize that, to achieve this objective, we must use our resources efficiently, and we must provide for the proper balance among the fundamental obligations that we have to our shareholders, employees, customers, consumers, suppliers and within the society in which we operate.

In seeking to balance our desire for probable growth with the obligations that we have to our other various constituencies, we shall:

I. Protect and enhance the Corporation's high level of ethics and conduct.
• Honesty, integrity, fairness and respect must be key elements in all dealings with our employees, shareholders, customers, consumers, suppliers, and society in general.

- Our operations will be conducted within regulatory guidelines and in a manner that does not adversely affect our environment.
- We continually strive to be good neighbors and to support community projects.
- Employees are encouraged to take an active part in improving the quality of community life.

II. Maintain a strong "people" orientation and demonstrate care for every employee.

- Employees will be treated with respect, dignity and fairness.
- Employees will be given the opportunity to participate in and contribute to the Corporation's success.
- We strive to provide attractive, competitive wages and benefits, good working conditions, and reward for results.
- We pursue our sincere commitment to our Affirmative Action Program in the letter and spirit of the law.
- Promotion from within the Corporation is practiced to the fullest extent possible.
- We constantly strive to improve two-way communication at every level and to work with each other in a spirit of constructive cooperation.

III. Attract and hold customers and consumers with products and services of consistently superior quality and value.

- Our ongoing objective is to provide quality products and services of real value at competitive prices that will also insure an adequate return on investment.

IV. Sustain a strong "results" orientation, coupled with a prudent approach to business.

- We strive to attain challenging objectives to insure a steady rate of real growth, while maintaining the financial strength of the Corporation.
- We pursue profitable growth by maintaining excellence to our current business.
- Growth opportunities are actively sought from within and without the Corporation in areas that capitalize upon our strengths.
- We constantly strive for positions of market leadership.
- We shall continue to create a climate throughout the organization that causes this philosophy to become a way of life.

✦

JOHNSON & JOHNSON'S CREED

— We believe our first responsibility is to the doctors, nurses, and patients, to mothers and all others who use our products and services.

— In meeting their needs everything we do must be of high quality.

— We must constantly strive to reduce our costs in order to maintain reasonable prices.

— Customers' orders must be serviced promptly and accurately.

— Our suppliers and distributors must have an opportunity to make a fair profit.

— We are responsible to our employees, the men and women who work with us throughout the world.

— Everyone must be considered as an individual.

— We must respect their dignity and recognize their merit.

— They must have a sense of security in their jobs.

— Compensation must be fair and adequate, and working conditions clean, orderly and safe.

— Employees must feel free to make suggestions and complaints.

— There must be equal opportunity for employment, development and advancement for those qualified.

— We must provide competent management, and their actions must be just and ethical.

— We are responsible to the communities in which we live and work and to the world community as well.

— We must be good citizens—support good works and charities and bear our fair share of taxes.

— We must encourage civic improvements and better health and education.

— We must maintain in good order the property we are privileged to use, protecting the environment and natural resources.

— Our final responsibility is to our stockholders.

— Business must make a sound profit.

— We must experiment with new ideas.

— Research must be carried on, innovative programs developed and mistakes paid for.

— New equipment must be purchased, new facilities provided and new products launched.

— Reserves must be created to provide for adverse times.

— When we operate according to these principles the stockholders should realize a fair return.

◆

SCHNUCKS
THE FRIENDLIEST STORES IN TOWN

We are committed to excellence as an innovative retailer of quality foods, drugs, consumable products, and services. We focus on providing value through quality, variety, service, competitive pricing, and friendliness.

Our customers are our most important asset and must receive our total effort toward their satisfaction.

We must achieve profits above the industry average to maintain leadership and provide for future growth.

We shall employ and promote only the best people available, consistent with our organizational needs. We expect all associates to be competent and customer oriented. We will identify and recognize superior performance and will promote from within whenever practical.

We will conduct our business by treating all customers, associates, suppliers, and the community with honesty, fairness, respect, and integrity.

(Schnucks, Inc., is a large-scale regional food retailer with headquarters in St. Louis, Missouri.)

NOTES

1. *Time* (May 25, 1987): 14–29.

2. Sherwood Ross, "Unethical Conduct Is Rarely Reported," Reuters News Service, *St. Louis Post Dispatch* (June 5, 2000): BP4.

3. Diane Stafford, "Work Time Is Eaten Up by Online Time," *Kansas City Star* (December 9, 1999): C1. See also John Galvin, "The New Business Ethics: Cheating, Lying, and Stealing—Technology Makes It Easy. Get Used to It," *Smart Business for the New Economy* (June 2000): 88–99.

4. "The State of Greed," *U.S. News and World Report* (June 17, 1996): 62–68.

5. Sue Shellenbarger, "Workplace Upheavals Seem to Be Eroding Employees' Trust," *Wall Street Journal* (June 21, 2000): Bl.

6. Parts of this section were drawn from concepts included in the following papers presented at the Arthur Andersen & Company Conference on Teaching Business Ethics, held in St. Charles, Illinois, on June 18–20, 1989: (a) Robert Allen Cooke, "Business Ethics: A Perspective." Dr. Cooke was director of the Institute for Business Ethics at DePaul University. (b) John E. Fleming, "Principles of Business Ethics." Dr. Fleming was professor of management at the University of Southern California.

7.For more detailed discussion of ethical theories and models, see Laura Pincus Hartman, *Perspectives in Business Ethics* (Chicago: Irwin/McGraw-Hill, 1998), 4–59; and John W. Dienhart, *Business Institutions and Ethics* (New York: Oxford University Press, 2000), 95–143.

◆

3
—

Practical Guidelines for Making Better Ethical Decisions in the Workplace

Raymond L. Hilgert

What Is an Ethical Situation?

In the previous chapter, we discussed a number of schools of ethical study and an ethical model that can be related to situations that confront people in the workplace. However, many individuals experience difficulty even in identifying or recognizing ethical situations they encounter. Many prefer to use an ostrich approach and ignore the situation; they explain that they are not part of the problem if they stay out of it. In business and the workplace, Christians often are confused by mixed signals that come from their bosses, fellow employees, customers, and others. Rather than identify and try to deal with ethical components that are present, they frequently take short cuts, give in to the strongest pressures, or try to excuse what they do or don't do by saying, "It's none of my business" or "They made me do it." These dodges may provide an excuse, but they hardly are in keeping with the Judeo/Christian level of ethical behavior.

ETHICS IS NOT THE SAME AS COMPLIANCE

Abortion

Faced with conflicting priorities, some rely upon a simplistic definition of ethics: "As long as it's legal, its okay." This means that they rarely get past the Legal/Compliance level of behavior shown in Figure 2–1. They seek guidance from attorneys or higher level managers, such as human resource directors. They believe that, by relying upon such authorities, they are removed from the ethical consequences of what happens, even if they find that the "authoritative" advice and actions are contrary to their own sense of values. Some may not seek guidance; they prefer to rely upon the old premise "Everyone else is doing it and getting away with it." This, too, may be contradictory to what they know to be lawful or ethical.

These convenient rationalizations are among the most common misconceptions about the distinction between legality/compliance and ethics. Figure 3–1 depicts the contrast between the two, with ethics and ethical behavior going considerably beyond a solely compliance-based mentality. This urges all of us to practice much higher levels of ethical behavior rather than just doing the minimum necessary to comply with laws and regulations.[1]

Fig. 3–1

Compliance and Ethics

COMPLIANCE	ETHICS	
• The "letter" of the law	• The "spirit" of the law	*Matt 22:15-22*
• Doing things "right"	• Doing the right "things"	*Matt 12:1-8*
• Doing only what we "must"	• Doing all that we *matt 19:* "should"	*16-26*
• Rules	• Values - *Matt 19:16-26*	
• Policies (*contract*)	• Codes (*behavior*) *Matt 5:28-52/19:3-12*	
• Conformance	• Choices - *Matt 29:24-26*	
• Concerned (about law)	• Caring (for people)	*Matt 7:10-13* / *Mk 3:1-7*

In general, compliance with laws or regulations should be viewed only as a starting point. The Ten Commandments are as applicable today as they were in the time of Moses. But, as Jesus shows in His exposition of the Law of God in the Sermon on the Mount (Matthew 5–7), people try to fool themselves that they are pleasing God and earning salvation by a merely external keeping of the commandments. A follower of *Confession &* Jesus will be filled with the Holy Spirit through the *Absolution* Word of God and the Holy Sacraments and will go on to lead a life of continual repentance while obeying the spirit of the Law and developing a Christlike demeanor in thought, word, and deed. And when failure comes, as it often does, the Christian will find forgiveness through confession and Absolution and from the Sacrament of the Altar.

FEATURES OF ETHICAL/MORAL SITUATIONS

Ethical situations and dilemmas are part of our daily lives—in family, society, and the workplace. They arise so constantly that we may not be aware when a certain situation actually involves a moral choice. Figure 3–2 shows the features of ethical/moral situations.[2]

Fig. 3–2

Features of Ethical / Moral Situations

- Involves the interests / values of others
- Involves my interests / values
- Requires my judgment
- Requires my action / non-action
- Affects my life and the lives of others

In business, most decisions involve the interests and values of numerous parties. The Christian needs to be sensitive to the ethical dimensions of the situation. This means to have a kind of spiritual antenna, which defines and assesses ethical and moral dilemmas. It means to have an organized, practical framework by which to make decisions that are of the highest ethical quality and are Christian in nature.

Here follow two sets of practical guidelines by which ethical situations can be systematically dealt with. Having a process that can be applied consistently and appropriately should lead to decisions that are ethically sound.

A MODEL
FOR ETHICAL DECISION MAKING[3]

Over the decades, many books, classes, and seminars on principles of management have included a systematic approach for solving problems and making decisions. In recent years, these models have been adopted and adapted by ethicists.

OBSERVATIONS ABOUT PROBLEM SOLVING
AND DECISION MAKING

Virtually all human activities involve solving problems and making decisions. This process comprises defining problems and then selecting a course of action. Many problems recur in business and the workplace; for many of these, there are policies that serve as guidelines. However, when confronted with new and unfamiliar situations, people find it difficult to decide on an appropriate course of action. This is especially true when the situation has ethical considerations.

It should be apparent that there has to be appropriate action, implementation, and follow-up in order for any ethical decision to accomplish the desired objectives. Using a structured approach does not preclude one from using intelligence, creativity, and unique applications to solve problems for which there are no easy answers. While many ethical situations and dilemmas require sound judgment and even intuition to solve, it helps to have a structured approach by which to confront the problem.

Fig. 3–3

An Ethical Decision-Making Model

Step 1: Determine the facts of the situation.

Step 2: Identify the ethical issues in the situation.

Step 3: Specify whose interests are involved and who will be most affected.

Step 4: Develop a list of available and realistic alternative solutions.

Step 5: Analyze the ethical impact and implications of each of the alternative solutions.

Step 6: Select the solution that provides the optimum ethical resolution.

Step 7: Implement the decision, follow up, and adjust if necessary.

AN ETHICAL DECISION MAKING MODEL

Figure 3–3 depicts the principal steps of an ethical decision making model. It represents a logical process that should lead to an ethical decision. Each step within the model will be elaborated upon in the section to follow.

STEP 1: DETERMINE THE RELEVANT FACTS OF THE SITUATION.

First identify the key facts and factors of the situation. Rank the principal factors by priority, that is, decide which you consider to have the most impact and which are of lesser importance. This should enable you to designate who will be responsible for deciding and acting. This first step may indicate that there are gaps in the information available and that it is necessary to search out additional information before moving on.

STEP 2: IDENTIFY THE ETHICAL ISSUES IN THE SITUATION.

Too often there is a desire to make a quick decision rather than making sure that there has been adequate analysis. According to an old adage, "Nothing is as useless as the right answer to the wrong question." This certainly is applicable to ethical decision making, because if the ethical issues have been incorrectly or only partially identified, solutions that are developed will be lacking in quality.

It is useful to separate ethical issues from other issues that are part of the total situation. Some issues may be broad and part of the total situation; some may be organizational or business-related; some may be personal in nature; others may involve conflicts between various individuals or groups.

STEP 3: SPECIFY WHOSE INTERESTS ARE INVOLVED AND WHO WILL BE MOST AFFECTED.

This step often is close to step 2. Some authorities use the term "primary stakeholders" to determine the key individuals or groups who will be most affected. This step involves answering pointed questions. Whose interests are involved? What would be the consequences of action or inaction? What criteria can be applied to help specify fair treatment to individuals who are part of the situation?

STEP 4: DEVELOP A LIST OF AVAILABLE AND REALISTIC ALTERNATIVE SOLUTIONS.

As a rule, any decision will only be as ethical as the best alternative solution. You must stretch your mind to develop alternative solutions that are conceivable, available, realistic, and capable of meeting desired ethical criteria. Among these should be reducing the amount of harm to others; maximizing benefits to the majority of others; acknowledging and respecting various conflicting interests; and being fair to individuals who will be affected by the decision. This can take time, but it is worth the effort. If a decision is needed quickly, such brainstorming may have to be accelerated. However, where time is available, it is desirable to consult with colleagues.

STEP 5: ANALYZE THE ETHICAL IMPACT AND IMPLICATIONS OF EACH OF THE ALTERNATIVE SOLUTIONS.

Each alternative must be evaluated in terms of how it will affect the individuals involved (i.e., the stakeholders). Alternatives must be assessed as to their ethical qualities using either (a) the ethical schools described in chapter 2 (e.g., utilitarian, rights, etc.); (b) the model of ethical levels (Figure 2–1); or (c) the applied tests for ethical decision making, which will be discussed later in this chapter. Diligent analysis will sharpen your focus and raise important questions.

STEP 6: SELECT THE SOLUTION THAT PROVIDES THE OPTIMUM ETHICAL RESOLUTION.

After analyzing all the alternatives, select the one that will provide the most of what is wanted and will eliminate or reduce to a minimum what is not wanted. It is necessary to consider all of the potential consequences to arrive at a choice that will be ethically best. This does not mean that the solution will be absolutely perfect in all respects. We live in an imperfect world, and many workplace and business decisions, no matter how carefully they are ethically crafted, will seem unfair. The best decision, however, should seek to maximize the benefits to the greatest number of people and reduce harmful consequences to others. Fairness should always be a major consideration, along with respect for the rights and dignity of others. Ask yourself what would be the God-pleasing thing to do.

WWJD?
Sanctification

If none of the alternatives appears to be optimal, go back through the steps of the decision-making process. There may be other alternatives that were not considered previously; it might be possible to combine some of the alternatives to develop new possibilities. At some point, however, you have to make a decision. Your solution may not be entirely satisfactory. But at least you can be comforted by the thought that you considered all conceivable ethical alternatives in a serious effort to treat everyone fairly.

STEP 7: IMPLEMENT THE DECISION, FOLLOW UP, AND ADJUST IF NECESSARY.

Implementation and follow-up of a decision are actually part of the decision-making process. It frequently occurs that when a decision is put into place, events do not follow the blueprint that had been developed. It therefore becomes necessary to make adjustments. This may mean making just minor changes or it may mean making major adjustments or even going through another step-by-step decision process.

Such evaluation should ascertain whether the decision achieved what was intended. It may require consultation with people affected by the decision and explanations to those who feel their interests were not adequately considered. Try as you might, sometimes even reasonable people disagree with your decision. This does not mean that such a decision was unethical. People will often view what was done from their own self-serving perspectives. This reality also includes Christians, redeemed but still struggling with the old sinful nature.

Throughout the decision-making process, numerous questions and checkpoints can be utilized in making better ethical choices. In the section to follow, we will identify some ethical guidelines that can be applied in conjunction with the step-by-step decision process or that may be applied independently to analyze contemplated courses of action.

SOME APPLIED TESTS FOR ETHICAL DECISION MAKING

The ethical decision making model (Figure 3–3) is a practical step-by-step mental process that works for many ethical dilemmas. It particularly is useful in solving complex problems in which the decision-maker needs to sort out conflicting areas in order to arrive at the best decision for all concerned. For Christians, it is a practical approach for striving to attain the Judeo/Christian ethical level (Figure 2–1); it can be adapted to numerous situations, both professional and personal. Unfortunately, in the pressures of the workplace, Christians often are influenced by considerations that blur moral distinctions and keep them from making the most ethical choices. Certain problems must be handled quickly, and time pressures prevent a careful decision-making analysis.

It is helpful to consider a number of ethical tests that can be applied quickly to alternatives. These can be utilized independently or within a structured decision-making process. The ethical tests can be useful to Christians in the workplace as they try to make choices consistent with the teachings of Scripture.

THE LEGAL/COMPLIANCE TEST

As discussed previously (Figure 3–1), the starting point for ethical decision making should be to make sure that any relevant law, regulation, or policy should be followed, not broken or ignored. The old saying "Laws are made to be broken" is false. The police won't accept the excuse, "Everybody's doing it."

Certainly, there are times when the application of a particular law or policy may be in some doubt. This is no time to rely solely on one's own biases and judgment or to take advice only from a boss or colleague who is no better informed than you are. It is prudent and more ethical to seek out guidance from someone who is in a position to know the proper interpretation. This could be a higher-level manager, the firm's legal office, the human resources director, or some other qualified person. Ignorance of the law is no excuse, and it is always a weak explanation for making a poor decision. However, to violate a law or regulation willfully, or to neglect to take an extra step to ascertain a proper interpretation, is quite unethical and also a glaring example of poor judgment.

Operating within the limits of legality or compliance is just an initial part of ethical decision making. Referring again to Figure 3–1, ethical choices tend to go far beyond just a compliance mentality. But as a starting point, the legal/compliance test is a necessity; it is crucial to the quality of a decision.

This Assumes the law is God honoring.

THE PUBLIC KNOWLEDGE TEST

Ask yourself: What would happen if my decision became known to the public? What would be the reaction if higher management found out? How would I explain my decision to someone I love, such as a spouse, parent, or child? If I would be comfortable explaining my decision to someone I love and to anyone in public office, higher management, or the media, the decision choice is probably of acceptable ethical quality. On the other hand, if the public knowledge test leads to discomfort or anxiety, this should be a strong signal that the contemplated choice is ethically flawed, and another alternative should be sought.

THE LONG-TERM CONSEQUENCES TEST

Consider the long-term and short-term outcomes of each alternative and weigh these adequately. Too often, individuals in business and the workplace make a choice that will lead to immediate short-term gains, such as more profitability, a higher bonus, more income, or some other presumed advantage. Time and again, people make short-term decisions that come back to haunt them in the future. This will never foster the stability and growth of a business enterprise. The long-term reputation of a firm typically is based upon the credibility and trust that have been built and nurtured over the years. Further, there is ample evidence that doing the right thing in business over the long term is more profitable and satisfying than just going for the fast buck. Not only is this the ethical thing to do; it also tends to be in the best material interest of the firm that hopes to build a solid foundation for relationships that will make it successful in the future.[4]

THE EXAMINE-YOUR-MOTIVES TEST

In this test you take a serious, introspective look at yourself. Are your motives to benefit the organization and others? Or are your motives primarily personal and selfish in nature, perhaps designed to harm or demean other people and their interests? Your own reputation can be destroyed if others perceive that your choices are always self-serving in nature. Nobody trusts someone who is totally absorbed in his or her own personal and business welfare and shows no concern for others.

THE INNER VOICE OR CONSCIENCE TEST

Perhaps this should be listed as the first test of ethical decision making, since it is the test of conscience and moral values, as informed by the Word of God. The conscience might be seen as the voice of God within each of us, speaking through the words of Holy Scripture and urging us to make decisions that are ethical and God-pleasing. We should listen to this voice and act accordingly. If you do not listen to your inner voice or conscience, a whole host of undesirable outcomes may follow. The inner voice test in and of itself may not always clearly indicate what is the right thing to do. Christians should constantly be studying the Scriptures.

94

Determining the most ethical choice may require a careful analysis. However, the inner voice test certainly can provide the necessary guidance to avoid making poor ethical decisions. If something inside you says that a choice being contemplated is wrong or that it may be wrong, usually it is wrong. Such a signal tells you to set aside the poor choice and look for different and better alternatives that will satisfy the inner voice and other ethical tests. Study the teachings of Jesus. Learn the letters of St. Paul. The more of the Bible you know, the stronger your conscience will be and the clearer your inner voice.

APPLYING ETHICAL TESTS MAY NOT ALWAYS BE SUFFICIENT

The diligent application of these ethical tests will usually lead one to make better ethical choices. In business and the workplace, what may seem to be the most ethical decision can be complicated by conflicting pressures that come from bosses, employees, customers, and others. In many situations, it will be necessary for the Christian to have ethical courage and seek advice from colleagues and those in authority before deciding what to do. Discussing ethical aspects of complex decisions in business and the workplace should not be viewed as passing the buck. Rather, it should demonstrate that making ethical choices is a priority concern for Christians.

QUESTIONS FOR DISCUSSION

Self - Satisfaction
look good before men
Easier

1. Why do many individuals contend that behaving ethically primarily involves compliance with laws and regulations? What does Jesus say to those who live by a surface compliance only? See Matthew 15: 3–11.

2. Review Figure 3–1 (Compliance and Ethics) and give examples for each of the comparisons within this illustration. Can you think of biblical examples for any of them?

3. Review Figure 3–2 (Features of Ethical/Moral Situations) and discuss why so many situations became ethical/moral dilemmas. What moral dilemma did Abram face in Genesis 22:1–18? What about the apostles in Acts 5:21–32? *- 1st Table vs 2nd Table of law*

4. Review each of the steps of the Ethical Decision-Making Model (Figure 3–3). In your opinion, which of these are the most crucial in ethically resolving a difficult problem or dilemma? Why? *3 ε 6*

5. The assertion was made that the ethical quality of a decision will only be as good as that of the best alternative. Do you agree or disagree with this concept? Why? How does 1 Corinthians 5:6–8 address this issue? *A little leven affects the whole loaf.*

6. The ethical tests discussed in this chapter were the legal/compliance test, the public knowledge test, the long-term consequences test, the examine-your-motives test, and the inner voice test. For each of them, try to cite specific examples of ethical dilemmas that you have experienced in your job, that you have learned about, or that have been reported in

the media. Discuss how application of one or more of these ethical tests could have brought about outcomes that were more ethical than what actually transpired. What is the final that that we will face? See Matthew 25:31–46. How does Ephesians 2:8–9 temper this test? *slave/goods*   *R. like* Humility

7. Which of these ethical tests do you find to be the most practical or appealing? Why? Will the inner voice test always provide a Christian with the needed guidance to determine the right thing to do? —NO Discuss. How does Philippians 3:12–4:1 direct our *Although* thoughts and decisions? *Guided by H.S. it wisdom of wise it is to be listened to and not using to break.*

CASE PROBLEMS

These case problems are based on classroom papers by students at the Olin School of Business of Washington University. (Names in the case problems are fictional.)

"Abusing the System," Beth Fogle-Bradford

"To Promote or Fire?" Lorry Luscri

"Searching for Employment," Jennifer Gundrum

▶ *Abusing the System*

Principal Characters:

Judy Harmon, analytical chemist

Neil Markus, supervisor, Analytical Chemistry Laboratory

Bob Petke, director, Analytical Chemistry Laboratory

Samantha Wood, administrative assistant

THE SITUATION

Judy Harmon worked in the analytical laboratory of a large chemical processing firm. One of her duties was to log in all incoming samples on the lab database. On a daily basis, she probably logged in about a hundred or so samples from throughout the world. Packages came in many different sizes and shapes, and they were not always addressed to her. Numerous packages were addressed to her supervisor, Neil Markus. For this reason, Judy was instructed to open all packages that came to the analytical laboratory. On one particular day, Judy opened a package that contained two pairs of designer khakis and two expensive-looking button-down shirts. Samatha Wood, who delivered packages to their final destinations within the company, happened to be walking by. "Hey, Sam," said Judy. "There must be some sort of mistake; these are clothes, not samples." Samantha replied, "No mistake. Neil ordered those through a catalog last week. The clothes belong to him." Judy figured that Neil must be getting some sort of good discount through the catalog, and she left it at that.

The following week during a lunch period, Judy heard Bob Petke, the lab director, telling Samantha Wood that he would like to see the "latest and greatest" catalogs. Judy thought to herself, "Hmmm, I wonder what sort of women's clothes these catalogs have?" At that point she confronted Samantha and asked her about the whole situation: "Hey, Sam, how does this work? We order items from the catalog, and then once they arrive, how do we pay for them? Do we just write a check out to petty cash?" Samantha replied, "Well, you see, Judy, that's not how it works. People are not paying for them. I code these orders out to the miscellaneous laboratory expenses account. Laboratory clothing, which includes lab coats, safety shoes, and safety glasses, falls under miscellaneous lab expenses. As the director, Bob Petke monitors what is spent on a monthly basis. Bob and Neil order personal clothes all the time; so do some other people around here. You know those fancy white shirts Bob always wears? Catalog! You know the nice pants that Joe always wears? Catalog! Bob's responsible for the laboratory budget, so obviously he doesn't see a problem with the whole thing!" Judy Harmon was appalled by what Samantha had told her, but Judy decided she would just "close her eyes" to this behavior and not make an issue of it.

Several months had gone by when upper management brought to everyone's attention a major cost-control program. The company was going through some tough times, and management urged everyone to curb unnecessary spending. Around the same time, Judy noticed numerous orders coming in not only for new labcoats but also for more pairs of khakis, shirts, pairs of Rockport "safety" shoes (second pair within the last six months), and even a pair of flannel-lined jeans for Neil. (Judy had never seen Neil wear jeans to work in the year that she had been there!)

It was obvious to Judy Harmon that company personnel were using company funds to purchase personal clothing. She felt that she must do something. She was uncertain how Bob and Neil could justify these expenses. Neither worked in the lab itself, so they couldn't claim that they were damaging their clothes at work. Being the director and supervisor over the analytical lab, Bob and Neil surely made enough money to buy personal clothes with their own money. Yet, Judy thought, if she blew the whistle on them, how many others would be found out and perhaps be hurt by the consequences? What if some of them were her closest friends? And would Judy herself be in trouble for not reporting her suspicions until several months after first having learned about what she realized was a scam? Maybe top management didn't care, because highly qualified and capable professionals like Neil, Bob, and others were difficult to recruit and retain. Judy wasn't even sure to whom she should report the problem. Maybe her best option was just to continue to keep her mouth shut and order some clothes for herself.

QUESTIONS FOR CASE PROBLEM

1. Identify the primary ethical issues in this situation.

2. Utilize the decision-making model and the ethical tests that were discussed in this chapter to (a) define alternatives that are open to Judy Harmon, and (b) evaluate the ethics of each of these alternatives.

3. If you were Judy Harmon, what would you do, and why?

speak the truth in love

4. How might Ephesians 4:15 guide Judy's decision? Why is it hard to determine what the most loving thing is?

▶ *To Promote or Fire?*

Principal Characters:

Paul Poag, store manager

Mark Worley, computer sales department supervisor

Jim Valli, recently hired salesman

Chad Yang, long-service salesman

THE SITUATION

Mark Worley supervised 10 salespersons in the computer department of an urban store belonging to Strategic Office Technologies, Inc., a chain store corporation. Mark reported to the store manager, Paul Poag.

Recently, the store's computer sales had slumped significantly. Paul called Mark into his office to tell him, "It is time to do something about it." Paul suggested that Mark should hire another salesman. Although Mark felt that the current salespeople were sufficient, he told Paul that he would comply with this suggestion.

After interviewing several candidates, Paul and Mark hired Jim Valli, a man with 12 years of previous computer retail sales experience. After Jim's first six weeks, Mark completed the mandatory probationary evaluation. Mark documented that Jim was adjusting well with the other employees and that his attendance and sales performance were commendable and exemplary.

About six months later, Paul Poag again called Mark Worley into his office. Paul showed Mark sales data that indicated that Jim Valli's sales were twice that of any of his co-workers. Paul commented to Mark how much Jim's performance was benefiting the company, and he suggested that Mark should promote Jim to a position as assistant department supervisor responsible primarily for the evening shift. Mark responded that he would consider this idea and decide in a few days.

Later that same day, Chad Yang, a salesman who had been a loyal and productive employee with the company for about 15 years, came to Mark Worley's office. The following conversation took place:

Chad: The grapevine tells me that you're thinking about promoting Jim Valli. This can't happen.

Mark: Why not? Jim has been outstanding. And how did you find out about this anyway?

Chad: Never mind that, but I also know that Jim Valli has a prison record in his background, and we were never told about that.

Mark: When we interviewed Jim, he was quite open and frank about his past. He got caught in a theft at a former employer over 10 years ago. He served his time, made full restitution, and has had an honest and clean record ever since. Paul and I decided that Jim Valli deserved to be hired because of his qualifications and experience;

what he had done in the past was over and done with. I'm surprised that you found out about this and that it should even be brought up as being a problem.

Chad: It's a really big problem with me and some of the other salespeople. We should have been informed about this earlier. None of us will ever trust him. Once a thief, always a thief! And the thought of him being a supervisor makes me sick to my stomach. I've served lots of years with this outfit, and you prefer to promote an ex-con who's been here less than a year.

Mark: You've been an excellent salesman for us, Chad, but you told me a few years ago that you preferred selling to becoming a supervisor.

Chad: Maybe so, Mark, but this situation is totally different. The bottom line is this. Either you terminate Jim Valli, or I'm leaving. Either he goes, or I go. There are others here who feel the same way as I do. It's that simple. We won't have any problem finding other positions.

Mark: I'm sorry you feel that way, but please give me a few days and we'll talk about this again.

Chad: Okay, but I'll only wait a few days for your decision.

Chad Yang then left his office. Mark Worley was still visibly upset when Paul Poag arrived unexpectedly at Mark's office door.

QUESTIONS FOR CASE PROBLEM

1. Identify the primary ethical issues in this situation.

2. Utilize the decision-making model and the ethical tests that were discussed in this chapter to (a) define alternatives that are open to Mark Worley, and (b) evaluate the ethics of each of these alternatives.

3. If you were Mark Worley, what would you do, and why?

4. How might Colossians 3:12–17 guide Mark? How can Mark deal properly with this situation among workers who are not Christian?

▶ *Searching for Employment*

Principal Characters:

Justin O'Neal, recent college graduate

Michelle Isam, college-student friend of Justin O'Neal

Stuart O'Neal, father of Justin O'Neal

THE SITUATION

Justin O'Neal had returned home in early May after graduating from State University with a B.S. degree in accounting. Justin had been accepted into the M.B.A. program at State University beginning in September.

Justin was anxiously hoping to work in the accounting or finance department of a local company. He had taken several interviews during the past two weeks, but he had received no job offers. Although he was well qualified, companies lost interest in hiring him when they found out he was only able to work for the summer. The company interviewers told Justin it was not worth their investment to train him if he was quitting in a few months, and they preferred having someone who would be able to work long-term.

Justin was particularly intent on finding a good job because his father, Stuart O'Neal, had been harassing him about the issue. Over the past three summers, Justin had worked at a swim club as a lifeguard. Justin could probably work there again this summer, but the lifeguard position didn't pay very well, and it would not provide him with professional work experience to list on his resume. Justin also was hoping to earn higher wages over the summer, because he needed enough money to pay for his books and tuition for the upcoming fall semester. His father had told Justin that he was too old to work at the swim club. Further, Stuart O'Neal had pressured Justin to find a job that would provide valuable experience to help him get a good job after he graduated with his M.B.A. Unfortunately, Mr. O'Neal had not been able to help Justin find a company that needed summer help in their accounting or finance departments.

Frustrated with his lack of progress, Justin discussed the issue with his steady girlfriend, Michelle Isam, who had just accepted a position as an assistant sales manager for a computer company. Michelle, too, was home for the summer after her junior year at State. Michelle told Justin that she did not tell the company interviewers that she would be returning to school in a few months. Rather, in her job interviews she had said that she was dropping out of State University for financial and other reasons and that she intended to complete her bachelor's degree at a local university on a part-time basis. That, according to Michelle, was how she got the job offer. Michelle said that several of her friends also had secured good summer jobs by using this same type of strategy.

Michelle suggested that during any future job interviews Justin should conceal his intention to return to State University in the fall. After all, she reasoned, many people resign after they begin working because they don't like the job. Michelle insisted that Justin wouldn't be hurting the company because he would be hired at will. It was Justin's right to quit whenever he wanted, just as the company could terminate him at any time. Besides, the company could just as easily hire someone who would wind up not liking the job, and that person might quit even sooner than Justin.

Justin had an interview scheduled for Wednesday. He had not mentioned to the firm's employment manager that he was still a college student or that he was just looking for a summer position. The employment manager previously had indicated that the company was looking for someone who would be a full-time permanent employee. Justin had listed on his application form the work experience he had gained in high school and college while working as a supervisor at a local fast food restaurant and his summer position as a lifeguard at the local swim club. Justin also listed his experience as an "assistant network consultant" at a small firm where he had worked part-time during the previous school year. Justin had greatly exaggerated the extent of his responsibilities and the number of hours he had worked, but he felt that "everybody did this," so no real issue would be made of it.

As he prepared for the interview, Justin thought about what Michelle had said. He knew that Michelle had been dishonest, and he felt guilty for exaggerating his credentials on his job application form. At the same time, he really wanted to have a good job, and this position was exactly what he was looking for. He didn't know how much longer he could listen to his father's complaining or how he would be able to earn enough money to pay for his graduate school expenses if he had to return to the swim club.

It was Wednesday morning before the interview. Justin felt rather uncomfortable as he debated with himself about what he should say to the job interviewer about his employment situation.

QUESTIONS FOR CASE PROBLEM

1. Identify the primary ethical issues in this situation.

2. Utilize the decision-making model and the ethical tests that were discussed in this chapter to (a) define alternatives that are open to Justin O'Neal, and (b) evaluate the ethics of each of these alternatives.

3. If you were Justin O'Neal, what would you do, and why? How does 2 Corinthians 3:1–3 deal with this issue?

NOTES

1. This illustration was adapted from ethics seminar training materials provided in 1991 by Mr. John Strickland, former vice president for corporate ethics at McDonnell-Douglas (now Boeing) Corporation in St. Louis, Missouri.

2. This illustration was adapted from materials used in a graduate school business ethics class at the Olin School of Business of Washington University as presented by Dr. Stuart Yoak, adjunct professor of philosophy (spring 2000).

3. This section was developed from principles and concepts discussed in a number of sources, primarily the following: Raymond L. Hilgert and Edwin C. Leonard, Jr., *Supervision: Concepts and Practices of Management*, 8th edition (Cincinnati: South-Western Publishing Co., 2001), 127–50; "The Seven-Step Moral Reasoning Model," presented at Arthur Andersen & Company Conference on Teaching Business Ethics, held in St. Charles, Illinois, June 18–20, 1989; "Ethical Decision Making," included in pamphlet, *Ethical Business Conduct Guidelines*, distributed by the Boeing Company (June 1998).

4. See the following articles: Hugh Aaron, "Do the Right Thing in Business," *Wall Street Journal* (June 21, 1993): A10; "How to Be Ethical, and Still Come Out on Top," *Economist* (June 5, 1993): 71; "Business Ethics: Doing Well by Doing Good," *Economist* (April 22, 2000): 65–67.

◆

4

Making Christian Ethics in the Workplace a Reality

JAMES L. TRUESDELL

We have looked at the Bible. We have discussed the various theories of ethics. We have discussed tests and criteria for evaluating workplace decisions from an ethical perspective. Now how do we apply these to the fast-paced pressures of the real world?

Theoretical discussions are fine, but in the working world we may encounter situations that call for rapidly made and irrevocable decisions and do not allow time for reflection and analysis. Bosses and workers will be called upon to react quickly, and the morality of their actions may well turn on whether they and their company have conditioned themselves to act within an ethical framework. Have they established a climate in which workers can and will do the right thing, even if it results in a short-term loss to the company? Is the worker who makes such a decision protected from career repercussions for the lost order or missed opportunity because he or she would not step over the line of propriety?

BUILDING AN ETHICAL CULTURE

Companies have personalities, which we popularly call "cultures." These dictate the way people go about their work, the way they relate to each other, the pride (or lack thereof) workers feel in their enterprise, and the sense of mission that exists in an organization. Cultures will tell us something about the extent to which employees feel ownership in an organization, the extent to which they will go the extra mile to meet the customers' needs, and the way a company interacts with and is perceived in its community or industry. A significant part of that cultural identity is determined by the level of ethics that exists at the enterprise. An organization with a strong backbone of ethical guidelines, be they specifically written out or merely understood, will attract the best employees, secure the quality contracts, and earn the trust of its customers. Likewise, it will pull along its employees and raise them to a higher level of ethical behavior as they emulate the organization's leadership and strive to live up to the company's reputation.

But whose responsibility is it to create an ethical culture? What can the Christian do if he or she is in the midst of a situation where right and wrong is not taken into consideration or, worse, where illegal, unethical actions or exploitation are the norm?

In chapter 2 we presented a number of established companies' ethical policy statements. This is certainly a starting point. Company management or the board of directors can be instrumental in developing such a statement. But this will be only so much window dressing if the reality of people's behavior is not consistent with the published policy. Worse, deviations from a public policy only heighten a perception of duplicitousness when actions are at odds with high-sounding rhetoric. The supposedly Christian company whose owner or employees regularly take the ethical low road bring scorn upon themselves and all believers. Those who ridicule the church are all too willing to pounce upon and highlight instances of hypocrisy among professing Christians.

In the small- to medium-sized business the owner-manager bears a unique responsibility to set the stage for morality. This CEO is often beholden to no earthly power but his customers, and he can provide the pattern that his organization will follow. If he is observed seeking fairness and avoiding exploitation, others will follow suit. If he is willing to run roughshod over workers, suppliers, the environment, or the community to achieve money or power, no one is surprised if his employees follow. To a lesser degree, the manager within a large public or bureaucratic enterprise faces the same responsibility. If she is willing to figuratively knife competitors in the back (whether they are within or outside the organization), then the message is being sent on down the line

1 Cor 6:17-20

Pastors belong to the Lord.

CEO-First belong to the Lord

that such is the way to get ahead in the organization. Someday some younger and hungrier person will step over that manager's body on the way to the top.

THE WORK ETHIC

Business success is indeed driven by the ambitions and desires for material success of entrepreneurs and people seeking to rise in their careers. This is the part of human nature from which our free-enterprise system draws its strength. This is not to be condemned, because material success allows a business to survive and to provide jobs, sustenance, and wealth for the community and the betterment of all.

In the story of Mary and Martha (Luke 10:38–42) Jesus speaks to the priority of the spiritual side of life versus daily chores. He is not condemning work per se, but is merely calling us to put it in its proper place and time. We are to seek the kingdom of God first (Matthew 6:33).

People who are in positions of leadership in business organizations need to reflect on whether they are driving themselves and their workers for pure material gain and self-aggrandizement or whether they are successfully channeling that ambition toward a larger goal based on service to the community and meeting some real needs of their fellow human beings. The place for a leader to begin that reflection is with his own motives. Jesus provides us the perfect example of servant leadership with His washing of the disciples' feet. He clearly demonstrates that the effective leader must be a servant, tending to the needs and comfort of those who follow. So must today's leader see himself as a servant of the workers, knowing that giving conscientious attention to people's problems and promptly providing resources and answers will translate into success for the enterprise.[1]

A number of years ago, in response to competition from the auto and electronics industry in Japan, American manufacturing companies began a widespread adoption of the techniques of Total Quality Management as taught by Edwards Deming and other management gurus. In addition to statistical process control and other measuring systems, goal setting, teamwork, and doing things right the first time were increasingly emphasized. The concept was that quality started from the top by leaders setting the example and then constantly communicating with and receiving feedback from workers on the front lines. Above all, leaders of the company must always have "quality" on the tips of their tongues. All decisions are to be made in light of the impact on product or service quality. All meetings are to have quality as part of the agenda. This concern for quality becomes contagious within the organization and workers buy in to this culture when they see their leaders taking it seriously over a long period of time.[2]

Cannot the same case be made for ethics? Does not the Christian business leader have an obligation to mold his organization's climate accordingly? If workers see the boss asking questions about the right thing to do when decisions are made, then they will be encouraged to follow the precepts of ethical behavior. Those who serve on corporate boards or controlling boards of charities and community service agencies can also use those opportunities to place ethics on the agenda and make it a component of decision-making.

CULTURE AND ETHICS

A group of managers sits around a conference table considering a new product marketing plan. Planned advertising and literature representations of the product will stretch the truth about the product's capability to its limits. Assertions will be made that it can outperform the competitor's product, but the group knows that such is the case only under a narrow set of conditions and circumstances. Someone asks whether these claims can get the company into any legal difficulty. The group discusses possible ramifications. Another manager asks what the competitor's likely response will be to the campaign and whether the risks of a counterattack would negate the hoped-for benefits. Spirited debate follows this question. At some point a junior manager speaks up and asks, "Is this really the right thing to do? Aren't we attempting to mislead our potential customers?" An embarrassed silence falls over the conference room. The senior VP of marketing finally says, "That's not really relevant. We're talking about increasing our market share here. If it's not illegal, I'm not worried about it." End of discussion.

A message has been sent. Raise ethical questions only if you want to be thought of as a naive fool. What if that senior manager is a professing Christian? Has she so thoroughly compartmentalized life that there is no room for God's rules at the office? What does it mean for that manager's ability to live comfortably with herself? What impact does this action have on other workers, who learn that they too must subordinate their principles to the win-at-all-cost culture?[3]

Imagine that that senior manager had responded with a simple acknowledgment: "Thanks for raising that, Steve. Maybe we have failed to look at what we really stand for here. Let's talk about how we could approach this in a way consistent with our company values." Henceforth others would feel comfortable raising such questions. The senior manager has set the ethical tone. She either possessed the wisdom and character to see this need on her own or has been conditioned to respond in this manner by the CEO and board. Unfortunately, the opposite is too often the case. The message is made clear that coming out on top is the only thing that matters, without recognizing that the company that sees this as the only goal will eventually pay a price in lost customers, loss of respect in the community and the industry, and dissatisfied managers and employees. They will realize that they have sold their souls to the god Mammon.

Let's suppose that you are a peer of the young manager who raised this uncomfortable question in the meeting. The silence ensues. What is the Christian's duty? Clearly it is to support the person who has put it on the line by raising questions of right or wrong. A simple, "Yes, that troubles me too," legitimizes the subject and validates the person who has raised it.

In recent years there have been Christians who urge us to ask ourselves continuously, "What would Jesus do?" when confronted with ethical choices. Of course Jesus is holy, but we are not. He is all-powerful, but we are not. So we cannot ultimately think or act like He would. Yet by the sacrament of Holy Baptism we have His Spirit within us. Christ lives in our hearts by faith. He helps us resist sin and be like Him in thought, word, and deed. So, in a sense, this is a valid way of evaluating our personal choices in the home and the workplace. Corporate culture and legal environments might prevent us from asking this question directly in many instances, but some variation is certainly appropriate in any situation. (An example might be, "How does this action measure up to our values, and is it consistent with the kind of organization we really want to be?")

The Christian employee will want to do everything possible to make the discussion of ethics legitimate in his or her workplace. Affirming an existing culture that does take this into consideration and helping others change their focus to think this way are subtle but powerful ways the Christian can witness to Christ's grace in our lives. Our work lives become a reflection of and testament to God's love.

THE CHRISTIAN'S DUTY

Many business issues do not lend themselves to black and white, clear-cut analysis. In many situations, mitigating factors can cause good or ill to come to various parties regardless of which direction is taken. For this reason we cannot set ourselves up as judges of others' actions or be intolerant of the legitimate views of others. Where Scripture and our Christian perspective tell us, however, that certain behavior is clearly unethical, we must not by our willing participation or silence condone such actions. Silence in the face of illegal or unethical conduct in organizations of which we are a part chips away at our own integrity, weakening our faith and our witness to others. We can rationalize our failure to act in terms of protecting our job and our family's security. But what have we gained if we protect our family's income, yet lose part of ourselves in the process? There comes a time when we must tactfully speak up or choose to leave the situation, lest we become stained by participation in actions with which we cannot agree. These decisions can be particularly painful for those who have invested many years of their career at a company or who, because of age, skills, economic factors, or geographic considerations, do not have a large number of alternative jobs available. The Christian worker, if he is true to his or her convictions, has a duty to respect authority, but his first duty is to God. We must be prepared to take risks with our career by making ethical choices. If this is difficult, remember that making unethical choices carries a far greater risk. God will protect His children in hard times.

Those in authority must be acutely aware of the impact of their actions on their subordinates. Christian business leaders would probably be surprised at how cynically their workers view their actions. This is due to the relative powerlessness that line workers feel. Leaders should recognize the ultimate equality of Christian people and the inherent dignity of all workers. They are entrusted with power over others' lives, and that power should be exercised with sensitivity and fairness.

The equality of Christian people can be experienced in a fully functioning and living church, where all parishioners are accepted regardless of economic station in life or position of power in the secular world. Here the walls of caste and pseudo-aristocracy come down as people study the Word and worship together. Too often, however, churches are divided by social and economic classes, with people deferring to those who are leaders in the secular and business world. Where this is happening, parishioners miss an opportunity to gain an appreciation of people's equality before the Lord, a perspective that can be carried over to the workplace. Diminishing one's fellow man or denigrating his contribution has no place in Christian ethics, which reflect Christ's sacrifice for us.

We spoke earlier of the eagerness of opponents of the church to find hypocrisy and inconsistency in the

Equality in the Lord / I Cor 10:11

actions of Christian businesspeople. For this reason, those who openly point to their faith must be especially careful that their actions measure up to the standards they espouse—and not just in their own minds. Think of the harm done to the cause of Christ by those high-profile media evangelists in the 1980s whose personal lives were racked by scandal and financial and sexual improprieties. Remember how they were mocked by network television comedians and secular journalists? Think how the stereotype of the televangelist cast a pall over the perception of many legitimate and dedicated Christian media personalities!

When we hold ourselves out as Christians in the workplace, we are setting ourselves up as examples by which the nonbeliever will judge the church, all other Christians, and by extension God's own reputation. The fact that the believer in Christ claims forgiveness and salvation cannot be perceived as a license to sin. The Christian who confuses self-interest with God's plan for his life can turn others off to the church. They won't agree that God has decided to favor the believer with success at the expense of the unbeliever.

The temptation to confuse self-interest with righ- *Temptation* teousness can be a particular problem for business owners or entrepreneurs because they live in an environment where no one acts as a check on their perception of reality. The business owner/entrepreneur sets the *←* rules, and employees learn to play by those rules or go elsewhere. Some egocentric personalities begin to say,

119

"What is in my interest is good and right, and what is not in my interest is wrong." The illogic in this view is readily seen by others who do have to operate in an environment where the wants and desires of others must be taken into account. What if this same self-centered individual also self-righteously holds herself out to be a Christian or, because of riches or social status, is accorded high position in the church? Significant harm can be done to the spiritual lives of those who quietly turn away from such hypocrisy. They can't separate the cause of Christ from those flawed human beings who are His followers. How much better for those blessed with high position to adopt an attitude of humility in Christ, acknowledging their shortcomings and focusing on servant leadership! A little self-deprecating humor helps, as long as it is genuine. This is an indication not of weakness but of strength, as we ask others to follow our lead and help them channel their efforts toward the organization's goals.

ACTING FOR THE COMMON GOOD

Similarly, a concern for ethics must focus on the common good, not just an eventual economic payback. The saying "Good ethics is good business" may well be true (though it is difficult to quantify the benefits of ethics in either the short or long term).[4] But if we accept this as our sole rationale—linking ethics to profits— then we may be freed from ethical restraints when a decision is perceived as not in the business's best financial interest. Such a statement implies that the basis for decision making is not ethics but a self-interest that just happens to be moral.

The concept of acting for the common good is paramount in all endeavors, says James Boldt, former executive director, Department of School Ministry, The Lutheran Church—Missouri Synod. As an educator, he believes that people in authority must be more concerned about the common good than they are about their own positions. He sees this concern as coming from values that we have an obligation to teach to our young people. One of these key values is the mutual obligation of employer and worker to deliver a good day's pay for a good day's work and vice versa. Other key values must be imparted to the new generation of workers:

1. Putting others' interests before your own.
2. Doing everything possible to help people meet their needs.
3. Showing care for others by doing for them what you would do for yourself.
4. Helping anyone and everyone in need, regardless of race, creed, or color.
5. Listening to others so that someone really hears them.
6. Working for justice and love for the unloved.
7. Challenging those in high office to deal honestly and fairly with all.
8. Empathizing with those who have no advocate.

9. Sympathizing with (but not pitying) those who need our sympathy.

There is a parallel in these values between meeting one's own needs and meeting those of the community and your co-workers and customers.

"This motivation is the hallmark of good business," says Boldt. "It is, in fact, a paradigm. It is simply this—when I help others I end up profiting. Inversely, when I look out for myself I end up failing. The whole thing is a paradox. If you want to succeed you must meet people's needs."[5]

There is, of course, a definition of success that is not tied so directly to profits or self-interest. It sees service to others as an end in itself—an end that is usually more satisfying than material gain. Right now we are reaping the harvest of the philosophy that having things is more important than treating other people with respect and dignity. The attraction of drugs and prostitution is easy money, as is the attraction of white-collar crime. One could add to this list gambling addictions and abuse of easy credit by people who are living above their means.

◆

SOME LARGER ISSUES

THE PROFIT MOTIVE

Underlying our free-enterprise system is the drive to create profits as return on equity. High-priced seminars and M.B.A. programs focus on teaching ways to increase profits through combinations of maximizing pricing and reducing costs. Since these actions usually have a negative impact on someone else (i.e., the consumer who experiences higher pricing and fewer services or product features or the employee who is "downsized"), we must ultimately ask, "When is enough, enough?" The laughing response of many businesspeople would be, "When I get one dollar more!"

Indeed, there is much to support the idea that profitability should be unlimited, that profits are the nutriment that feeds our economy, creates jobs, and solves problems. Our standard of living far exceeds that of socialist countries, which tried to abolish the profit motive. Socialism did not work. It seemed to kill the human spirit, especially when coupled with a Marxist philosophy that denied the existence of God and persecuted believers. Business profits can be a good thing. Is there a point, however, when the Christian must begin to reassess how that profit motive is being applied in his or her business and life? When profits are maximized because of inferior products, deceptive advertising, extortion-like pricing practices where supply is limited, or exploitation of workers through unfair wages or poor working conditions, then it is time to reassess what is going on. When the pursuit of profit becomes the prime motivation in a person's life, then his relationships with friends and loved ones and his spiritual life begin to suffer.[6]

One is reminded of Charles Dickens's *A Christmas Carol*, in which, confronted with the ghost of his partner Jacob Marley, a frightened Ebenezer Scrooge says, "You were always a good man of business, Jacob." To which the apparition shouts back, "Mankind was my business! Charity, mercy, forbearance, and benevolence were all my business. The dealings of my trade were but a drop of water in the comprehensive ocean of my business."[7]

When we consider what motivates us to work, we look at the world's reasons, which include love of money, necessity, fear, and duty. But the most soul-satisfying reason is to praise the Lord by serving our fellow man. As Jesus said, "What good is it for a man to gain the whole world, yet forfeit his soul?" (Mark 8:36).

HIGH STANDARDS AS AN ETHICAL IMPERATIVE

There is a sense of right and wrong in everything we do. There is a right way ... and there is a wrong way. A business and its people have an obligation to produce quality goods and services. Consider the Bible's admonitions with regard to our approach to our daily work: "Whatever you do, work at it with all your heart, as working for the Lord, not for men" (Colossians 3:23). "Whatever your hand finds to do, do it with all your might" (Ecclesiastes 9:10).

Quality and high standards may be said to have an ethical or moral dimension insofar as those who depend upon the organization (i.e., its clients and customers, as well as its employees) depend upon its survival. Its survival is a function of its goods and services.

Powell Woods, a Lutheran pastor who in his first career rose through the ranks to become vice president of human resources and community relations for Nestle, USA, says, "The primary moral obligation of any management team is to focus the employees of the organization upon quality and to assist them in every possible way to carry out the quality mission."

A true organization-wide dedication to quality and ethics does a great deal to improve the way employees feel about themselves. A large part of anyone's self-image is contingent upon how he feels about life at work. Work is, after all, quantitatively the largest single element in our lives. Most of us spend more time and emotional energy on our work life than on anything else.

The major responsibility for quality rests squarely upon the leadership of an organization. While it is possible for a raising of standards to come from within the ranks, it is certainly difficult without leadership. If employees remain unconvinced that their management cares about doing things right, then it becomes very difficult for them to pursue it in any meaningful way. This is a challenge for Christians in positions of leadership. They must set the tone. The worker contributes by putting forth his best effort and encouraging co-workers to do likewise.

Woods tells about what he considers one of his industry's greatest successes in sending a message about high standards and concern for the consumer. This occurred at Stouffer Foods, a Nestle operating company that had lost money every quarter in the early 1960s until they began to achieve a reputation for having the finest frozen food product in the marketplace. No expense was spared. Only the finest ingredients were purchased, and recipes were fine-tuned until they were just right.

"One time a huge bunch of macaroni was slightly overcooked," says Woods. "They could have gone ahead and used it, but management decided not to and they called the entire work force together around the 'kettle.' They made a little speech about the importance of product quality and then dumped the whole batch down the drain."[8]

It is this kind of demonstrated willingness to take a significant loss in order to maintain quality that drives belief in the concept home to the employees.

EMPLOYER-EMPLOYEE RELATIONSHIPS

Slaves, obey your earthly masters with respect and fear, and with sincerity of heart, just as you would obey Christ. Obey them not only to win their favor when their eye is on you, but like slaves of Christ, doing the will of God from your heart. Serve wholeheartedly, as if you were serving the Lord, not men, because you know that the Lord will reward everyone for whatever good he does, whether he is slave or free. And masters, treat your slaves in the same way. Do not threaten them, since you know that He who is both their Master and yours is in heaven, and there is no favoritism with Him. (Ephesians 6:5–9)

The idea of viewing the employer-employee relationship in a master-servant context seems a little odd in our modern world, where people move from job to job selling their services as a commodity. Yet there remains the basic relationship of the principal (employer) calling the shots while the agent (employee) carries out the orders and represents the principal. Having chosen to accept a particular job, the worker has a duty to help his company achieve its objectives. This means he follows directives, procedures, and work rules without complaint and gives his best effort to help the enterprise succeed. By accepting employment, he implicitly agrees to treat his employer with respect, speak no ill of him or her, honestly serve as a steward of company resources, and protect company customers, secrets, or proprietary information from the competition.

Things are changing in the world of work. People no longer plan to stay with one company for a career.

Workers may feel more loyalty to a profession than to the companies that provide jobs for that skilled profession. They may be more concerned with what the company can do for them than with what they can do for their company. They may be cynical about any efforts to promote company loyalty. They have grown up seeing their parents dedicate years of their lives to organizations only to lose their jobs to downsizing in their later years.

Does this change the Christian's duty to serve his company to the utmost of his ability? The answer is no. Employment remains a conscious decision and is a contract entered into by free will with certain duties inherent in its performance. "But if anyone obeys His word, God's love is truly made complete in him. This is how we know we are in Him" (1 John 2:5).

On the other hand, an employer purchases the labor of his worker. He does not purchase the laborer. At all times the employer must remember that each worker is a fellow child of God, beloved in the Lord's sight. Any dehumanizing treatment of a worker, such as considering her as merely a commodity or subjecting him to physical or emotional abuse, is inconsistent with our duty to love and value our fellow humans. Even a well-intentioned paternalism toward workers can be dehumanizing.

Any time a manager depersonalizes the worker he will eventually treat that worker unethically. For this reason, the owner-manager who is concerned with reflecting Christ's love in his workplace actions should look first to his thoughts and perceptions regarding workers, for these will most certainly be a precursor to action.

The ultimate test is the Golden Rule. An employer-employee relationship does not alter Christ's call for us to do unto others as we would have done unto ourselves. Within the context of the implied contractual duties that employment gives rise to on both sides, this is still the guideline.

CORPORATE CULTURE OR IDEOLOGY

We tend to think of business cultures in terms of large corporations. These entities exist unto themselves and are not the creation of a single individual entrepreneur who sets the tone for his workers. So we study the development of the corporate ethos that dictates how people within that organization will relate to one another, the customers, and the community.[9]

The corporation demands loyalty from its associates and requires a certain degree of commonality of belief from its workers if it is to achieve its goals. The repeated actions of its managers and workers over a period of time form a de facto ideology that helps to guide decision making. This can be something akin to the tests outlined in chapter 3. It can also be an aggressive, "push the envelope" philosophy.

Does the existence of a corporate ideology require the Christian to surrender his beliefs? Must you condone actions you disagree with if you are to advance?

Most corporate strategies or decisions of questionable propriety are those aimed toward short-term gains or profits. Actions are often taken that bring immediate profits to the company or make someone's financial statements look good at the expense of healthy long-term relationships with customers, employees, vendors, or other constituencies. This is not surprising because people are usually promoted for achieving short-term and immediate goals. Then they reach a position of high authority and are suddenly expected to take the long-term view as to what is in the best interests of the company.

Would it not be better to begin to voice the long-term view even as you rise within a company? Point out the impact on the company's future of shoddy products or borderline ethical practices. Even if overruled, you will have avoided surrendering your ideals and principles to expediency.

THE CUSTOMER IS ALWAYS RIGHT—RIGHT?

A truck driver in a hardware distribution business made his normal delivery run one morning, delivering construction material to a general building contractor. The contractor (the customer in this scenario) was waiting for the delivery. When the driver arrived, the contractor quickly gave the driver directions as to where he wanted the material unloaded in his shop, waving his arm in the general direction of an area at the rear. He was obviously in an agitated state and in a hurry as he headed out the door for an appointment. The truck driver spent about half an hour unloading the bulky material where he thought it was to go. Several hours later, the truck driver's employer got an irate call from that contractor complaining about "your stupid driver" who had unloaded the material in a place that blocked their work flow. He demanded an apology.

Eager to retain the contractor's business, the employer apologized profusely to the contractor and promised to speak to his driver. He did so and asked the driver to apologize to the customer when he made his next delivery. The driver, feeling he had been given inadequate instructions by the customer, fought the idea of apologizing. In his mind the apology was being given solely to promote the economic self-interest of the employer, and he was being asked to debase and humiliate himself by apologizing for something that was not his fault. The situation was finally resolved by some role-playing and careful wording whereby the truck driver would express his regret that the customer was inconvenienced by the material's placement and his assurance that he would be extra careful to get complete instructions next time. This seemed to satisfy the customer without forcing the driver to lie about his own culpability.

It is not unusual for customers to be insulting and demanding and to ask the unreasonable. Some people use the power position of purchaser to dangle others over the fire. Sometimes this may take the form of impossible or even illegal requests. Yet companies recognize that their employees must always treat the customer with respect. If each individual situation gives a worker the right to evaluate whether a customer has stepped over the line, then it is likely that some very bad judgments will be made, chaos will ensue, and a company's reputation for service will suffer. Better that employees be trained with a firm set of guidelines for how much leeway is granted in acceding to customer requests. And they need to know how to handle the unruly or demanding customer. There is a point, however, past which the customer is no longer right: no employee should be subjected to uncontrolled verbal or physical attacks or harassment by customers. Company management must be prepared to kiss that account goodbye if the customer cannot behave in a businesslike and ethical manner.

Remember, we are all consumers too. It is incumbent on the practicing Christian to set the example and love his neighbor even when that neighbor is a customer service rep who has lost a critical order, a service repairperson who fails to show for an appointment, or a telemarketer who makes a living by calling homeowners to hawk some home improvement service. In our daily work, we may be on the other end, and anything we can do to contribute to the overall civility and kindness in society will again be a witness to the faith that is working in our lives.

In the end, we are all called to serve. God has given

us a vocation, and we glorify Him by serving others with whom we come into contact. Be we consumer or provider, we are part of one economic community, with all the different players interdependent. The more oil we can personally apply to the gears of that community, the better the engine will work.

QUESTIONS FOR DISCUSSION

[handwritten margin notes: Examples, P.114, P.126 - Stouffer foods]

1. Think of the culture that exists at your workplace. Is it conducive to moral and ethical decision making? If not, what can you as a Christian do to help change that culture? How does positive change occur? See Matthew 13:31–33. *[handwritten: - A little leaven affects the whole loaf]*

2. Define what servant leadership means to you. What are the advantages and disadvantages of this style of leadership in a modern business enterprise? What does John 15:9–17 say about servant leadership? How can we avoid making servant leadership just another tactic for success? *[handwritten: P. 112; Jane Inglis's Book; Whole Being]*

3. What responsibilities do leaders have as stewards of their employees' work lives and efforts? Can Christ's example of sacrifice be likened to the task of the effective leader? Why or why not? Can a non-believer be a servant leader? What does 1 Corinthians 2:11–15 say about the nonbeliever? *[handwritten: P.126 - 128; Narrow & wide sense]*

4. Is the statement, "Good ethics is good business," really true? Is this sufficient motivation for ethical behavior in the workplace or is something else needed? Discuss. How does Matthew 6:33 apply to this maxim? *[handwritten: (P.112)]*

5. What does acting for the common good mean with-

"Family secret"
"Don't Rock The Boat"
"Cooperate & Graduate"

in the context of the community? The workplace? Is this synonymous with ethical behavior? Can you think of instances where it is not? Discuss Jesus' comments about "good" in Mark 10:17–18. How is God's idea of good different from man's concept of good? How does this apply to Romans 8:28?

6. What are the benefits to society of business profits? Is there such a thing as excessive profits? What does Hosea 12:2–8 say about God's attitude toward dishonesty in business?

7. What ethical duties arise between an employer and employee as a result of the employment relationship? What does Titus 2:6–14 say about the Christian context for work and the importance of a positive role model/corporate culture?

Acts 5:17

8. Does the duty of loyalty to the employer require a worker to adhere to a corporate ideology or ethos, even if, though not illegal, it is inconsistent with his or her personal or religious values? When would this be proper and when not? What does Ephesians 4:17–28 add to the discussion of Christian behavior in the workplace?

P. 130 f.

9. Is the customer always right? Is there a limit to how far we must go in agreeing with the customer and, if there is a limit, how can we tactfully draw that line without being disrespectful to that customer or disloyal to our employer? How might Philippians 2:12–18 guide the believer?

10. Discuss the application of the Golden Rule to workplace situations. What do we do when dealing with someone who does not reciprocate and takes advantage of us? The Golden Rule is part of God's Law,

not the Gospel. What does it mean to live by grace? See Romans 6:23.

CASE PROBLEMS

▶ *Political Involvement*

Principal Characters:

Sue Johnson, loan officer for a metropolitan-area commercial bank

Steve Ranken, president of the bank

Creighton James, chairman and owner of the bank

THE SITUATION

First Community Bank of Metropolis is a leading lender to the business community. The bank maintains a very high profile in the city and contributes money and the volunteer time of its officers to many charities and civic causes. The bank encourages its officers to give their time and occasionally gives them time off to go to meetings and special events. Sue Johnson has been an officer for eight years and is very well respected by her peers and management. She is also a committed member of a local evangelical Christian congregation. Her church takes a very strong pro-life position and is outspoken against the abortions being performed at a local family planning agency in the city. Every Saturday morning, the church's pastor and a number of the parishioners join other protesters to carry signs and picket in front of the agency's clinic. While there have never been any incidents of violence, the picketing draws the attention of local media and does often create some tense moments.

One Saturday Sue joined the picketers and, as luck would have it, was sought out by a local television station interviewer and candidly expressed her strong pro-life views. Bank owner and chairman Creighton James was watching the news that evening and saw Sue stating her views. Monday morning he received a call from a large depositor who happened to be a longtime friend. This friend had recently worked on a fund-raising drive for the family planning clinic. He angrily complained about Creighton letting one of his bank officers picket and verbally condemn the clinic. Creighton called up bank president Steve Ranken and ordered him to draw up a policy outlining limitations on the involvement of the bank's officers in political or controversial causes that might reflect negatively on the bank or alienate bank customers.

Steve drew up the policy and, though he himself was also strongly pro-life, called Sue in and informed her that she would have to end her public involvement in the protests. Sue felt this was an infringement of her rights of free speech. She also felt she had a duty to speak up against abortion, which she considered to be a violation of God's Law. Steve told her that if she refused to comply, he would have to terminate her employment. Sue has worked hard to get to her current position. She is a widow and still supports her two high-school-age children living at home.

QUESTIONS FOR CASE PROBLEM

1. Identify the primary ethical issues in this situation.

2. (a) What alternatives are open to Sue Johnson? (b) What can Steve Ranken do to resolve the situation?

3. Can you think of other sensitive moral or religious issues that could present the same kind of problems? How did Peter and Paul deal with their conflict? See Galatians 2:11–21. *homosexuality, creation vs evolution*

Prayer in school, life issues,
Dress codes,

▶ *The Sloppy Installation*

Principal Characters:

Dave Smithton, product manager for a wholesale air conditioning distributor

Bill Jones, self-employed air conditioning contractor and a regular customer of Smithton's distributorship

Sam Pagesi, owner of a new residence where Jones has installed a heating and air conditioning system

THE SITUATION

Sam Pagesi and his wife recently moved into their home in an expensive <u>new</u> subdivision. After several weeks living in the house, Sam and his wife continued to experience very uneven distribution of the air conditioning in the new home. Some rooms were very cold, and others (especially the upstairs master bedroom) got very little airflow and were not cold enough. Additionally, the system was quite noisy with the sound of air rushing through the ducts and a periodic humming sound. After Sam complained to the builder, heating contractor Bill Jones came out and made several repairs and adjustments. After three such visits and modifications, all to no avail, Jones asked Dave Smithton, the distributor who sold him his equipment and supplies, to come out and see if he had any ideas.

Smithton came to the house and immediately saw that the system had been negligently designed and installed by contractor Jones. To remedy the situation, Smithton knew that not only must the air conditioner and furnace be ripped out and replaced with larger units but also some of the walls would have to be cut open to replace inadequately sized ductwork. When Smithton told Jones what must be done, Jones reminded Smithton of how much he purchased annually from his distributorship. He said he had no intention of changing out the system and would just tell Sam Pagesi that there was nothing wrong with the system. He cautioned Smithton not to say anything. At that moment Sam Pagesi came up to the two of them and, looking at Smithton, said, "Well, Mr. Expert, what did you find out?"

QUESTIONS FOR CASE PROBLEM

1. Identify the primary ethical issues in this situation.

2. (a) What alternatives are open to Dave Smithton?

(b) What should he do if, additionally, he believed the installation raised a risk of fire or explosion in the furnace? 5th commandment

3. If you were Dave Smithton, what would you do? How might 1 Corinthians 6:1–8 guide a decision about filing suit? Does it completely prevent lawsuits for believers?

Paul's Appeals
(Acts 9:2, 16:37,)
(22:25, 25:11)

Rom 13:1

church use court
to pass laws
to defend unborn,
Protect battered
woman, stealing
for homosexuality

▶ *The "Thank You" Trip*

Principal Characters:

Orville Thomas, buyer of ball bearings and other supplies for an independently owned motorcyle manufacturer

Cheri Swenson, regional sales manager for the nation's largest manufacturer of ball bearings

Ted Blanton, sole owner and president of the motorcycle manufacturer employing buyer Orville Thomas

THE SITUATION

Orville Thomas has been buying large quantities of ball bearings from Cheri Swenson's company for many years. The bearings are of the highest quality, come at a competitive price, and are delivered in proper quantities just in time for use in the motorcycle manufacturing process. Cheri has come to respect Orville as a good and knowledgeable buyer whose suggestions for product improvement have occasionally been incorporated into the bearing company's designs. Because of her company's respect for Orville, and in appreciation for his business over the years, Cheri invites Orville to a special "buyers' advisory council" meeting with some other large purchasers.

The meeting will be held in Miami Beach at the same time as the Super Bowl. Orville is invited to bring his wife. They will spend four days at a beach resort and will be seated in a private box for the big game. All of this will be at Cheri's company's expense. Orville will attend "council meetings" two mornings during the trip. Ted Blanton, owner of the motorcycle company and Orville's boss, is a big football fan, and his wife loves to travel. Two days before the trip, Orville mentions offhandedly to Ted about the council meeting he will be attending. Ted thinks to himself, "Hey, wait a minute. That's my money Orville is spending on ball bearings. Why wasn't I asked to go?"

QUESTIONS FOR CASE PROBLEM

1. Identify the primary ethical issues in this situation.

2. What would be a proper course of action for Cheri Swenson? For Orville Thomas?

3. In what situations would such a "thank you" be appropriate and ethical? How might 1 Peter 4:12–19 guide behavior and action? What does the Gospel of forgiveness say?

NOTES

1. James M. Childs, *Ethics in Business: Faith at Work* (Minneapolis: Fortress Press, 1995), 73.

2. James L. Truesdell, *Total Quality Management: Reports from the Front Lines* (St. Louis: Smith-Collins Company, 1994), 110.

3. Gerald E. Ottoson, "Essentials of an Ethical Corporate Climate," in *Doing Ethics in Business*, Donald G. Jones, Ed. (Cambridge, Mass.: Oelgeschlager, Gunn & Hain, 1982), 162.

4. George W. Forell and William H. Lazareth, *Corporation Ethics: The Quest for Moral Authority* (Philadelphia: Fortress Press, 1980), 23.

5. Truesdell, 193.

6. Clarence C. Walton, *Ethos and the Executive: Values in Managerial Decision Making* (Englewood Cliffs, N.J.: Prentice-Hall, Inc., 1969), 216.

7. Charles Dickens, *A Christmas Carol* (New York: Simon & Schuster, 1967), 52.

8. Truesdell, 42.

9. Michael Novak, "Can a Christian Work for a Corporation? The Theology of the Corporation," in *The Judeo-Christian Vision and the Modern Corporation*, Oliver Williams and John Houck, eds. (Notre Dame, Indiana: University of Notre Dame Press, 1982), 170.

✦

5

Moments of Truth—
Meeting the Ethical Tests

JAMES L. TRUESDELL

Every day we are faced with the temptation to take the easy road. Almost every action we take or decision we make has an ethical dimension. Will we choose to act in such a way that we are taking unfair advantage of another? Will we give less than our best to customer or employer? Will we make choices that we know in our heart are inconsistent with God's directives in our lives?

In this chapter we will look at some specific situations that confront Christian businesspeople. In most instances, an objective analysis can only lead a Christian to one obvious conclusion—there is a right way to handle the situation. But almost all of us must honestly confess that we have taken other directions at times. We have applied situational ethics to rationalize our actions, which just happened to enhance our own position. Each time we are presented with such a dilemma, we are reminded that a worldly price must be paid by those who adhere to God's Law. Our solace is that our ultimate reward lies not in the world's riches but in God's gift of grace. It recalls the parable of the rich fool and the admonition that worldly treasures are of little value to one who is not right with God (Luke 12:16–21).

A good guideline for evaluating these situations can be found in the steps outlined in chapter 3 (the public knowledge test, the long-term consequences test, the examine-your-motives test, the legal/compliance test, and the inner voice test). Most important to us as Christians, however, is the inner voice test—that is, heeding our conscience and measuring our actions against God's standards as written in the Bible. Though it is a higher standard than society and human law would require, this is the witness we are called to make to the world, showing by example that Christ's love guides our hearts.

In light of this, let us look at a series of problems, situations, and dilemmas that periodically raise their heads in our world of work.

THE ILLEGAL OR UNETHICAL ORDER FROM YOUR SUPERIOR

Let's say you have received an order from your boss. He asks you to falsify a record of the date of purchase of material so that a factory warranty will apply to a favored customer's claim of defect. When faced with a questionable order, an employee might ask the following questions:

1. Is it really wrong to carry out this order, or am I imposing my own values or self-righteousness on the situation?

2. Will anyone be harmed if I carry out this order?

3. Will the integrity of systems or procedures designed to protect against ethical lapses be compromised if I follow this order?

4. Will my duty be fulfilled by asking for a signed, written directive from my superior?

5. Will I look back and regret not refusing to carry out this order?

6. What would Jesus want me to do?

Where dishonesty is involved, the voice of conscience telling us that something is amiss must lead us to draw a line in the sand. If we do not, then we pull ourselves into a web of deceit that will haunt us and lay the groundwork for future misrepresentations.

When Peter and John were commanded by the elders and rulers in authority in Jerusalem to stop speaking and teaching in the name of Jesus, they replied, "Judge for yourselves whether it is right in God's sight to obey you rather than God. For we cannot help speaking about what we have seen and heard" (Acts 4:19–20). Just as it was apparent to the disciples then, there are some times now when the orders of those in authority are superseded by God's Law. Our task is to know when that point has been reached and then have the courage to tactfully decline compliance.

SETTING WAGES—AVOIDING EXPLOITATION

If you are an employer and business owner, you have the responsibility of paying a fair wage to those you hire to carry out your work. To successfully operate your business you must control expenses and ensure that your prices remain competitive. If you do not do this, the business will fail and your workers will be unemployed. But do you control expenses by imposing a low salary on an employee who has little other alternative, just so you can maximize profit? When does this become exploitation? Does our Christian faith require us to look beyond what we can negotiate?

If we as Christians are to look out for the interests of our brothers and sisters, then we must approach this by asking:

1. Is there any semblance of equal bargaining power? If a prospective employee has no other options, then the employer may have to go beyond self-interest to be truly fair.

2. Is the wage being imposed significantly below the market wage being paid for similar jobs in the area for people with similar skills?

3. Is there full disclosure of what is expected? If a significant part of the compensation is based on commission or performance bonuses, has true and valid information about past performance and market potential been provided?

4. Is the employee viewed mainly as a tool or asset—or recognized and thought of as a fellow human being?

5. Is there a sense of partnership in the enterprise, or is it more like a master-slave relationship?

6. How would you wish to be treated if you were the employee? Apply the Golden Rule (Matthew 7:12).

Christian duty does not compel us to give the store away and pay such exorbitant wages that we are at a competitive disadvantage with other companies. It does mean that we must take the interests of our workers into account in determining the fair day's wage for a fair day's work. We cannot operate in a moral vacuum when we are in a position of power over others. In the long run, fair treatment of workers will pay dividends in loyalty and the best efforts of workers who know they are important and valuable to the company's strategy. "The worker deserves his wages" (1 Timothy 5:18). "So I will come near to you for judgment ... against those who defraud laborers of their wages" (Malachi 3:5).

DEALING WITH PRESSURES FROM A CUSTOMER

Some of the toughest ethical problems arise when a customer tries to enlist us in questionable behavior. This can include offers of kickbacks or bribes to obtain priority service or extras (unknown to your employer), collusion in deceiving an end-user customer, and even asking for falsified or duplicate records to cheat the taxing authorities or some other party. This can be especially difficult because your refusal to go along may mean you will lose that customer. He will either shop for another supplier with fewer scruples or, because of embarrassment, simply avoid future contact. The temptation can be strong to seek a middle ground that will show "cooperation" with the customer. But just as you cannot be a little bit pregnant, so you cannot be a little bit unethical. If you engage in any unethical behavior, you become culpable in the entire action. What then to do?

Some possible responses:

1. Seek alternatives to help the customer: "We can't do that, but we can help you cut your costs by keeping those items in stock for future delivery."

2. Point out the legal risks. Your customer may have no moral code but will understand the threat of fine or jail. Allow the customer the "out" that he was probably unaware that the proposed act is illegal. Most people do not want to be perceived as crooks. Let him back off and save face.

3. Don't preach to the customer, but do stand your ground. There is a good chance that, with a tactful refusal to participate, you may still get the business. You might even cause that customer to rethink his or her behavior. You never know.

   "A wicked man accepts a bribe in secret to pervert the course of justice" (Proverbs 17:23).

AWARENESS OF THEFT BY A CO-WORKER

An employee's duty is to be a steward of company resources—to guard, protect, and responsibly use those assets in furtherance of the business's profit-making mission. What if you become aware of a co-worker's embezzlement or theft of inventory or cash? Is it any of your business, and is it betraying a fellow worker if you bring this to light? What if the whole culture at a company has begun to condone widespread and consistent stealing? Hard as it may seem, we do our fellow workers no favor by ignoring, covering up, and enabling continuing dishonesty. Further, by withholding information from our employer we become accessories to the drain on company resources. Our duty as an employee calls upon us to take some action that might include the following:

1. Directly approach your co-workers and state clearly that what they are doing is wrong and not consistent with company values. Assure them that you have higher expectations of them and that you expect them to stop the behavior and return the material. If they do not take immediate action, tell them you feel obligated to go to management. Follow through.

2. If that does not work, fulfill your duty as steward and inform the supervisor. This should be undertaken without a spirit of spite or malice toward the offending employee. It is merely an upholding of ethical standards at the workplace.

In either instance, pray that your actions are based on solid information and that your motivations are directed to the best interests of company and co-worker. The company expecting its employees to be forthright in protecting company assets must create an atmosphere that clearly communicates expectations of honesty and integrity among its employees. When a worker confides that misappropriation is occurring, he must be provided anonymity and protection from repercussions. Where dishonesty is allowed to exist without check it will soon spread to others within the organization. The result is a poisonous atmosphere that breaks down trust and chips away at the spiritual health of all.

From the standpoint of management's responsibility, active theft prevention programs send a message to the workforce that the company is seriously interested in regaining or maintaining control of its destiny and that it will set, implement, and execute policies designed to promote honesty. When a company suffers internal theft and no steps are taken to address the problem, employees may begin to ignore management suggestions and directives in other areas. When a company ignores theft, it reduces the ability of honest employees to fight off efforts of the dishonest workers to steal outright or to justify what they are taking as wages in kind.[1]

Oftentimes, when a prevention program is begun, one of the first results is that honest workers come forward to provide information to investigators. They often state that they are relieved that management is showing determination to bring permissiveness to an end and stop neglect that has allowed theft to continue unabated. The overall effect on *esprit de corps* is positive where efforts are made to stop theft that had previously been tolerated.

"The righteous detest the dishonest; the wicked detest the upright" (Proverbs 29:27).

OFFICE POLITICS

Jockeying for position within the office hierarchy, currying favor with the boss, and promoting one's image within the organization have become a science to which books and seminars are dedicated. That may be a part of business today (and probably always has been), but it can be carried to extremes. When it takes the form of setting up co-workers for a fall, highlighting the failure of a rival, taking credit for others' work, gossiping, or casting others in a bad light, then it becomes destructive rather than positive career building.

Ultimately, one who builds his or her career by stepping over the bodies of others will be found out. If that day of reckoning is somehow postponed, then the success will ring hollow to others and probably even to the person who has achieved it. Self-promotion that relies on tearing down others is the antithesis of Christian care and concern. When self-promotion is compounded by exaggeration, misrepresentation, and the intent to gain advantage over one's fellow workers, it is totally inconsistent with all that characterizes a good leader. One who aspires to be such a leader cannot afford to practice these destructive habits. In Paul's second letter to the church at Corinth he expresses his concern over what he might find when he arrives: "I fear that there may be quarreling, jealousy, outbursts of anger, factions, slander, gossip, arrogance and disorder" (2 Corinthians 12:20). Let us strive to keep our workplaces free of such practices, even as Paul urged the church to repent and humble itself before God.

CUTTING CORNERS ON SAFETY AND THE ENVIRONMENT

Over the recent decades, society, through legislative direction and court interpretation, has repeatedly expanded the scope of responsibility of business enterprises to provide safe products, safe workplaces, and environmentally sound work practices. Though legitimate debate exists over whether some of this regulation has gone too far and is counterproductive, there can be no doubt that every worker in every enterprise bears a responsibility to see that these rules are followed. Though some of the extra steps and procedures may be bothersome and expensive, they nevertheless are rooted in the need to protect ourselves, our co-workers, the company, and consumers.

If we are lax in adhering to these standards and procedures, we are putting someone or something at greater risk of harm than would otherwise be the case. Though we might cut corners and no one would be the wiser, doing so is a form of dishonesty that has potential repercussions to others. What if the safety rule you are ignoring threatens only your own health or well-being? The fact is that you have an obligation to your employer to minimize the risk of lost time, worker's compensation costs, and the company's investment in your training. There is little we do in the workplace that does not affect others. So—wear that helmet and safety harness!

In the environmental area, we must respect and care for God's creation. The Christian sees the world as God's handiwork and gift to us, a gift that we have an obligation not to defile. The Christian business owner and worker will take the lead in caring for the physical environment. "In the beginning You laid the foundations of the earth, and the heavens are the work of Your hands. They will perish, but You remain; they will all wear out like a garment. Like clothing You will change them and they will be discarded. But You remain the same, and Your years will never end" (Psalm 102: 25–27). "Holy, holy, holy is the Lord Almighty; the whole earth is full of His glory" (Isaiah 6:3).

DISCRIMINATION

Treating people differently based on subjective stereotypes or learned prejudices reflects the worst in all of us. Not only is it unfair but it also wastes the skills and talents of many people who could make significant contributions to our businesses. Much progress has been made in opening up opportunities to African-Americans, Hispanics, and other minorities. Still, we Christians must examine our hearts to ensure that the love of Christ is reflected in our attitudes toward and treatment of all with whom we come in contact.

There are some industries where old prejudices still prevail and employment, advancement, and business opportunities are still ruled by an old boy network. Those who have the power to do so can take an activist approach to bring diversity to their companies. Not everything can be legislated. People's hearts and minds cannot be won over by fear of litigation or regulatory sanctions. If we are to become a more tolerant and loving society, we cannot just wait for greater inclusiveness to evolve. We must take the initiative. Consider that Christ never hesitated to include among His followers those who were different or despised by the majority. Can we not follow His example? "If you show special attention to the man wearing fine clothes and say, 'Here's a good seat for you,' but say to the poor man, 'You stand there' or 'Sit on the floor by my feet,' have you not discriminated among yourselves and become judges with evil thoughts?" (James 2:3–4).

INTERGENERATIONAL CONFLICT IN THE WORKPLACE

Just as technology brings new and efficient methods to industry, so is there a constant regeneration of ideas, energy, and enthusiasm as each new generation joins the workforce. Every new group of workers brings its own unique outlook to the business world, growing out of the cultural and economic environment existing during their formative years. New theories and schools of management and different approaches to basic skills send them into the world of work with different expectations and ways of approaching problems.

Invariably, there will be abrasive encounters as the impatience of youth rubs up against the resistance to change of those who have successfully built the business. Unchecked, these conflicts can immobilize a business. Talented young workers will feel frustrated at the inability to have their ideas considered, while older workers will feel threatened and unappreciated by their younger cohorts. What is needed, of course, is a healthy dose of tolerance and understanding on both sides. Restraint and words of recognition and appreciation for each other can be a start to breaking down barriers. Will you be the first to take these steps?

"Rise in the presence of the aged, show respect for the elderly and revere your God" (Leviticus 19:32). "Don't let anyone look down on you because you are young, but set an example for the believers in speech, in life, in love, in faith and in purity" (1 Timothy 4:12). "Do not rebuke an older man harshly, but exhort him as if he were your father. Treat younger men as brothers" (1 Timothy 5:1).

EGO—KEEPING OURSELVES IN PERSPECTIVE

Many people need to be perceived as omniscient, all-knowing, and always correct. This is especially true in our competitive business world. To one like this, every action in your daily life is carefully orchestrated to portray yourself in the best light and to win the praise and admiration of those around you.

In time, this need to be superhuman can take over. What begins as a method of propping up your insecurities becomes a false persona that continually forces you to seek triumph after triumph to feed the monster of a grandiose self-concept. You step out of reality to become the ideal you are seeking. Not only does this make you difficult for others to relate to but it also diminishes others with whom you work, who must somehow assume a subordinate position because there is no room for two top dogs.

What you are doing, of course, is placing yourself in the position of God. Who needs the Lord's help if you have all the answers? How can you praise God in your daily life if you are too concerned with garnering praise for yourself? Is this a weakness with which you struggle? Ask God to help you put yourself in the proper perspective. Keep your eyes and heart on the Lord. Your best efforts in your job will gain you the admiration and respect you desire, but you will not feel it as a need. You will be freed from the tyranny of constantly needing to feed your ego. "You shall have no other gods before Me" (Exodus 20:3). That includes oneself!

MANAGING OTHERS—YOUR WITNESS IS SHOWING

The leader of a management seminar once cited a conversation with an executive who complained that his workers were presenting him with so many problems that he was developing an ulcer. This seminar leader scoffed at such a situation. "Bosses shouldn't get ulcers, they should give ulcers!" He then went on to extol the virtues of keeping employees in a constant state of fear as a means of extracting the most productivity out of them.

Whether this style of management is effective in the short term is open to debate. We should not deceive ourselves into believing that it is consistent with Christian care and concern. No amount of twisted logic can justify creating an atmosphere where people are constantly on edge and fearful of losing their jobs or being humiliated in front of their colleagues. Clear and consistent direction, consequences for failure to meet responsibility, and a clearly demonstrated passion for excellence are hallmarks of good management.

Those who rely on abuse of their fellow man, operating from a power position as business owner or manager, have to stop and ask themselves just what they are trying to accomplish. Is whatever success they believe they are achieving worth the misery they impose on others? If they are professing Christians, do they realize the negative witness they are providing to the world?

Referring again to Dickens's *A Christmas Carol*, we are reminded of the character of Old Fezziwig, the kind and benevolent employer of Ebenezer Scrooge in his early years. Thinking longingly back to his early days and the kindnesses shown to him by Fezziwig, Scrooge says, "He has the power to render us happy or unhappy; to make our service light or burdensome; a pleasure or a toil. Say that his power lies in words and looks; in things so slight and insignificant that it is impossible to add and count 'em up; what then? The happiness he gives is quite as great as if it cost a fortune."[2] As employers and managers we have the power to greatly impact the quality of our workers' lives. Let us use that power wisely and with kindness. What better way to witness the power of the Lord's grace in our lives!

WITNESSING BY OUR LANGUAGE

Some businesses and industries seem to have an approach to speaking which condones or even encourages "salty" language—graphic sexual slang, cursing, or taking the Lord's name in vain as a means of showing that you are one of the gang. Once this kind of behavior was typical of the "men-only" work environment, but now more women use curse words or foul language than ever before. In addition, there is the negative influence of the entertainment industry. Normal social and business interactions are frequently portrayed by sexual double entendres, careless exclamations like "Oh, God," and jokes about bodily functions.

Despite the prevalence of this behavior, many people—not only Christians—are put off and embarrassed by such conduct. Others are made uncomfortable because they somehow feel compelled to partake in such repartee even though they would not think of speaking in such a manner in the presence of their family or Christian friends outside of work.

Unfortunately, the use of such language can be contagious. The more it is used, the more it is picked up and imitated by others. Most of us want to feel that we are accepted by our peers. We are afraid of having others think we are judgmental, "holier-than-thou" prudes who put a damper on what they believe is normal behavior.

So what do you do when your work group or your customers engage in such talk repeatedly? You shouldn't "take the bait" and join in. To do so would be to validate such conduct and make you untrue to yourself. You could begin to develop bad speech habits which might spill out later at an inappropriate time. You certainly don't have to participate. That doesn't mean to excuse yourself or avoid contact with these people. Once you feel comfortable and familiar with co-workers it would be quite proper and appropriate to express your reservations tactfully to them. You can say that such language is unnecessary and not the way we as a company want to represent ourselves to the world.

If you are a boss or supervisor and are a believing Christian, have you examined your own communication style to see if you are free of this problem? Do you insert the curse word to add emphasis to your commands? Remember that what you do will greatly affect the culture of your company or department. Make your example one you would be proud for your children, spouse, or pastor—not to mention your Savior—to see!

"Above all, my brothers, do not swear—not by heaven or by earth or by anything else. Let your 'Yes' be yes and your 'No,' no, or you will be condemned" (James 5:12).

RESPECTING THE TIME OF OTHERS

There are many ways in which we show respect and concern for others in the workplace, but perhaps none more visibly than the manner in which we show that we value others' time. As an employee this means that we meet deadlines, fulfill assignments, show up for meetings on time, and carry our fair share of the load in projects. It means we avoid unnecessarily interrupting those engaged in projects or complex work. It means that we share resources with others, understanding that our personal work is only one component of the company's mission.

The manager or supervisor who keeps his workers waiting for instructions or authorization to proceed is failing in one of his prime duties—to keep the work process flowing. But he or she is also demonstrating that the workers' time is just not very important. This is bad enough when it is a result of poor time management or negligence, but there are those managers who seek to establish their own power by showing how little they value the time of workers or fellow managers. Insisting that others stand around waiting while they finish some task, refusing to allow meetings to proceed until they tardily arrive, or abruptly leaving if another is delayed for a minute—these all are intended to send the message that one is more important than his compatriots. It is placing more importance on primacy in the company pecking order than on the work or project to be done.

Each of us might take time to examine our actions in this regard. In the name of assertiveness are you grandstanding to build yourself up at the expense of others? If you are the boss, are you allowing some prima donna to act in such a manner and thus undermine the time and dignity of the majority of your staff? If you are the business owner and treat your workers so lightly, do you then have a right to expect them to give you the best use of their time in all other functions of the job? "Show proper respect to everyone. Love the brotherhood of believers, fear God, honor the king" (1 Peter 5:17).

DEALING WITH DEBT—
OWING AND COLLECTING

A business runs on cash. Financial managers pay a great deal of attention to cash flow management. The money manager who successfully brings in the cash and holds onto it is an important player in a winning company's management. Leveraging debt to produce the greatest return on capital invested is a science studied in business schools and analyzed by consultants. But does this too have an ethical component? Is the decision to delay payment past the due date smart business, or is it using others to accomplish our own ends?

In the construction industry it is not uncommon for building owners or general contractors to hold up payment to subcontractors for inordinately long periods. This produces a hardship on the subcontractors. These are usually small businesses dependent upon quick turnover of funds to pay workers and material suppliers. Likewise, some insurers drag their heels on settlement payouts by presenting technical hurdles and documentation delays, which allow them to hold on to their customers' money for weeks. Some businesses may follow a strategy of holding off payment until just before legal action or collecting agencies come into play. Others may run up debts and then try to negotiate a settlement for payment with a discounted amount, accepted by the creditor who desperately needs the cash.

The integrity of our word is at issue when we, or our businesses, purchase goods with a promise to pay. Buying with the intent to avoid our obligation or to use the other party's money without service charge or interest outside of the normal credit terms is a form of dishonesty. Sometimes circumstances arise after the fact; financial difficulties make payment difficult, and normal credit penalties (i.e., service charges or interest) apply. Likewise, those who are creditors must act fairly in seeking to compel payment for debts. While we have a right to expect the debtor to live up to his word and make repayment, neither should we lend upon usurious interest rates or use unscrupulous collection tactics.

"Let no debt remain outstanding, except the continuing debt to love one another, for he who loves his fellow man has fulfilled the law" (Romans 13:8).

UNFAIR USE OF THE COURTS

Our courts, attorneys, and legal institutions exist to provide a forum for peaceful resolution of disputes. They provide a valuable service when conflicting interests cannot be resolved by compromise or negotiation. Their very existence can even provide an impetus to settle disputes, lest the cost and burden of litigation be undertaken.

In an ideal world, they would continue to fulfill this role. Unfortunately, too often today we see those who abuse the courts with unnecessary and frivolous litigation. Parties are sued in what amounts to legal extortion, with the plaintiff hoping for an unjustifiable settlement just so the defending party can avoid the cost and time involved in defending. This has the further effect of raising liability rates for everyone and ultimately raising the prices of goods or making some goods or services unavailable. And yet access to the courts is an important right that can provide some equity and balance when the little guy is up against big corporations or powerful interests.

With such a powerful tool at our disposal, should we not exercise it judiciously and with restraint? Does not the Christian have every obligation to seek fair, negotiated solutions before using the lawsuit as a club to bludgeon the other party? In recent years Peacemaker Ministries of Billings, Montana, has been very effective in finding Christian solutions to human conflicts of all kinds. In this context, Mr. Ted Kober of Peacemaker Ministries has particularly emphasized the efficacy of the ancient, formal Christian rite of confession and Absolution.

"What you have seen with your eyes do not bring hastily to court, for what will you do in the end if your neighbor puts you to shame?" (Proverbs 25:8).

"Settle matters quickly with your adversary who is taking you to court. Do it while you are still with him on the way, or he may hand you over to the judge, and the judge may hand you over to the officer, and you may be thrown into prison" (Matthew 5:25).

SELLING WHAT YOU BELIEVE IN

Be it a service or product, successful selling is based on meeting a customer's need or resolving his problem. The most effective salesperson is the one who is truly convinced that his offering will deliver that solution.

Selling something that you cannot believe in yourself draws you into a dishonest relationship with your customer. If you intend to represent a company, examine what it is selling and satisfy yourself that you can wholeheartedly endorse it. An analogy can be drawn to the Christian's witness for Christ. The more grounded you are in your own faith, the more effectively you can tell the story to others.

The Christian salesperson represents not only his company but also himself and all that he stands for when he makes representations to his or her customers. He will take great care to see that promises are kept and that the company backs up its products. The best salespeople see this as a matter of sacred honor—they know that their integrity is the most important thing they are selling.

"Kings take pleasure in honest lips; they value a man who speaks the truth" (Proverbs 16:13).

WORKING FOR A COMPANY WITH A HARMFUL PRODUCT

There are certain industries whose products make us very uneasy. Their products can bring harm from improper use or even the intended use. And yet many good people are employed by and earn their living from these companies. Tobacco companies, liquor companies, retail outlets and printing companies involved in pornography, some elements of casino gambling, entertainment with questionable program content—what does the Christian do when he or she is part of such an enterprise? Indeed, is it right to even continue in that employment? The answer can be difficult, not only because of our economic dependence on the income generated but also because in some instances there is a clear socially and morally acceptable use for the product. Perhaps, as with alcohol or tobacco, it is only when abused or improperly used that the product or service is harmful.

Where such a proper use is present or possible and a Christian worker chooses to continue in employment, there is then an opportunity to influence that company to reorient its marketing, develop less harmful products, or to confront the problems caused by its business and attempt to minimize their impact. For example, note the many "responsibility" advertising campaigns launched in recent years by beer and liquor companies. If the harm is just one component of the company's business (i.e., a grocery store selling pornographic magazines), then the decision maker at that company can be lobbied to discontinue this unnecessary and offensive activity.

Whatever the decision, we should always be honest with ourselves about what is going on. If we delude ourselves as to the real nature of what the business is doing because we do not choose to face an uncomfortable fact, then we perpetuate the wrong and remove pressure on the owners to refocus their company. If a company providing a harmful product starts up a minor subsidiary or develops a small niche product with a good societal benefit solely for the purpose of covering its real mission, it is doing no better than Al Capone did when he operated soup kitchens for the poor in depression-era Chicago. The Christian worker must not delude himself about what is going on, even as the consumer must be aware of what he is supporting with his purchasing dollars.

"Submit yourselves, then, to God. Resist the devil, and he will flee from you" (James 4:7).

MAKING TOUGH DECISIONS— WHEN BAD NEWS CAN'T BE AVOIDED

There are times in the life of every business when actions must be taken for the good of the organization, but they are disastrous for some persons within the company. Sometimes if the company is to survive or if it is to continue healthy growth, certain divisions or offices must be closed. Sometimes workforces must be downsized. Sometimes it is necessary to terminate the employment of a well-meaning but nonproductive employee. All of these actions have very real human repercussions on the people affected and their families.

If you are involved in the decision-making process, you may find it necessary to act for the greater good and proceed with the unpleasant task. But by all means recognize the impact it will have! People's livelihoods and well-being are at stake. There are those individuals who seem to get a rush out of being the executioner. Wielding such power over people can feed their feelings of mastery and, at least in their eyes, enhance their power position among the survivors, who tremble as they wonder where the ax will drop next. Those who worship power can sometimes make a cult hero out of the individual who cold-bloodedly separates one person after another from the company.

We recognize the necessity for such moves and even the positive role downsizing has played in the resurgent U.S. economy. But delivering terminations free of remorse for the suffering caused and free of concern for the individuals affected does not fit the profile of Christian care. This situation calls upon us to prayerfully consider the options available, to undertake any reasonable measures to soften the blow, and to summon up every ounce of compassion and tactfulness we possess. We may well be casting our fellow believer into a situation where hard times will try his and his family's faith. We cannot for our own comfort erect a shell around our own feelings as we deal with this without risking hardening the heart of the person with whom we are dealing. He or she needs not only our love and empathy at this time but also our prayers now and in future days. Someday we ourselves might be on the receiving end. It is a chance for faith and love to be demonstrated by both parties.

"This is what the Lord Almighty says: 'Administer

true justice; show mercy and compassion to one another'" (Zechariah 7:9).

When Fiduciary Duties Conflict with Conscience

A "fiduciary" is one who is entrusted with a special role of stewardship to care for the property or interests of another. It gives rise to a very specific set of duties to exercise due care and prudence, honesty, and propriety in managing this interest. Fiduciary duties arise in such positions as trustee, attorney, corporate director (responsible for shareholders' interests), real estate agent, executor of estates, and a whole host of relationships that place one in relatively unsupervised control of the interests of others.

What happens when the dictates of our conscience place us in conflict with the interests of one to whom we owe a fiduciary duty? Short of illegality, it would seem that we cannot place our own interpretation of right and wrong in front of the duty we have taken to watch out for the interests of another. To do so would mean that we are betraying the trust we willingly accepted. When we act as a fiduciary, our obligation is to put our client's interest first. Thus, in acting as attorney or real estate agent, our first duty is not to reach a deal that is easiest or makes everyone happy; it is to procure the best results for our client, consistent with fair disclosure and honest dealing.

PROFESSIONAL CODES OF ETHICS— WHOM DO THEY PROTECT?

Among the sources of ethical guidelines discussed in our earlier chapters, many professions either informally by tradition or formally through their associations set forth rules for conducting business and customer relations. Most of these are inspired by the best interests of consumers. On the other hand, sometimes they are aimed at preserving the profession, maintaining its financial opportunities, and making it difficult for new competitors to enter the field. Those who develop and abide by such standards need to be honest with themselves and the public about the motivation behind such rules.

An example might be a local trade organization whose members got into the business by moonlighting from other jobs, working out of their garages or pick-up trucks, and utilizing a secretarial answering service during the day to field prospect calls. Once the business is developed and they are operating out of fixed offices with full-time staffs, they band together with other established contractors to "protect" the public interest by pushing legislation to require those in the trade to possess certain equipment, parts inventory, full-time offices, and other assets generally unavailable to start-up companies. The effect is to deny potential competitors the same route to success that they enjoyed.

Professional and trade standards can be a very

good thing, protecting the public interest. But those who promote them must be honest enough with themselves and others not to confuse ethics and 'the public interest with self-interest of their current practitioners.

THE FAMILY-FRIENDLY WORKPLACE— EMPLOYER DUTY, EMPLOYEE TRUTHFULNESS

Americans are working longer hours. As the "new economy" roared into life during the 1990s and U.S. productivity pulled farther and farther ahead of the rest of the world, it became increasingly clear that we were putting in more and more time on the job. Rather than providing additional leisure time, new technology was merely allowing people to work around the clock with an electronic tether attached.

At the same time, the women's movement and the high cost of living brought many mothers into the workplace. The resulting call for flexible work policies brought about legislation such as the Family Leave Act. Businesses saw that, to attract and retain quality workers, they would have to adopt family-friendly practices, which could range from flex-time schedules to on-site day care.

Indeed, if a company in today's competitive environment expects to demand long hours and high performance from its associates, it will have to help the workers handle some of the work/home conflicts that arise. This is not only good business but also a sane approach to time management. Too often workplaces are ruled by an atmosphere of artificial, macho competition, with managers vying to show who can work the longest hours or make the biggest sacrifices of family and personal time. This often has little relation to productivity, and the net result is family disruption at the expense of career.

If you are caught up in such a competition, will you have the courage to end it, or at least not contribute to its perpetuation? The wise manager will know when it is appropriate to put in the time (e.g., when deadlines demand it) and when it is done just for show.

Conversely, employees can take advantage of their company. Sick leave, time off for funerals, time management for outside salespeople and other salaried employees—all these carry the potential for the worker to improperly deprive the company of time and efforts for which it pays. Honesty and truthfulness in stewardship of this time is an ethical test to be confronted. Sick time is for sickness. Funeral leave is for funerals. Business time is not to be regularly used for personal errands. The fact that you can probably get away with something doesn't mean that you should. Listen to your conscience and follow its advice.

WITHHOLDING INFORMATION FROM OTHERS

The secret to negotiating is securing the most complete information. The theory is that if you have some information unknown to the other party, you will have an advantage and be able to get the better deal. This is perfectly logical if one adheres to the ever-popular "business is war" model.

Certainly it is important to know with whom you are dealing and whether they would be likely to withhold significant information. Nothing in the ethical realm calls upon us to be suckered in by someone who is trying to take unfair advantage of us. We must, unfortunately, be wary in our business dealings. But where is the line between wise negotiating and taking unfair advantage? What if we have knowledge that so radically alters the nature of the deal that the other party cannot fairly negotiate? An example might be an impending real estate development, known only to one party, which will multiply the value of real estate several times. Another might be a stock transaction in which only one party knows about a pending merger or acquisition. All buyers have the burden of making a reasonable investigation into facts surrounding their proposed purchase. But where access to information is unfairly limited, then they are obligated to tell the other party.

This can carry over to posturing and promoting oneself within an organization. Have you ever seen a person purposely confuse others or make information unavailable just to put others at a disadvantage? Have you seen someone ask questions at a meeting when they alone already know the answer, only for the purpose of verbally shooting someone else down in front of others? This kind of behavior is sometimes born of an ultra-competitiveness that sees everyone, even co-workers, as rivals. More often it is a result of insecurity, where someone seeks to bolster his own fragile position by falsely setting up someone else.

Our legal system has been evolving over recent decades toward a "no surprises" principle in litigation. Once, the lawyer who could engineer something unexpected could trip up his opponent. Now, expanded rules of discovery force out all evidence, witnesses, and, to a large extent, strategies. The idea is that the trial process is a pursuit of truth, not legal gamesmanship. The Christian approach to business and negotiating follows this same idea. Honesty and openness should be its hallmark. This requires a balance of caution and trust, but calls on us to err on the side of trusting if we are to lead by example.

"Do not trust in extortion or take pride in stolen goods; though your riches increase, do not set your heart on them" (Psalm 62:10).

TEAMWORK AND COOPERATION—BEING A SERVANT TO YOUR FELLOW WORKERS

In today's workplace, management often promotes team projects and divides the organization into work teams. This may well be a means of drawing together individualistic workers with little sense of loyalty to the company's larger mission. It also allows the blending of different talents and viewpoints to produce a better end product.

The Christian who interrelates with his fellow workers in a team, or just in everyday tasks, has the opportunity to demonstrate his servanthood to others by supporting and building up those with whom he works. Far from using the team as a forum to show off or dominate others, she can use this as an opportunity to draw out the contributions of those hesitant to speak up, to mend fences where rivalries have existed, and to help provide resources and assistance to others.

In everyday transactions we can view our co-workers as internal customers. This concept means that we view the person within our organization who receives the end product of our work as a customer. Just as we would with a regular customer, we learn to listen carefully to this person's needs and requirements and then deliver the work to them in such a manner that their needs are met and they can proceed to their own task.

This "internal customer" practice helps companies develop quality improvement processes. Each person is challenged to make substantive and measurable improvements in service to his internal customers. Internal customers, the recipients of work products, may be subordinates. This can be a great leveling experience. Managers learn to meet the needs of their assistants and buyers learn to meet needs of production line workers. It can be unsettling to the senior executive to have the tables turned—but it drives home the idea of servant leadership from a secular perspective. As a Christian in the workplace, can we not adopt this mindset in all of our interactions?

THE CALL TO CHRISTIAN LEADERSHIP

People have a fascination with strong leaders. In politics, business, and civic organizations we admire the goal-directed, decisive person who can get things done. There is even a seeming willingness to overlook the faults of, or even admire, the unethical person who steps on others on the way to the top.

The problem with the application of Christian ethics to business is that we often approach that application in a timid manner. As we agonize over whether to speak out and take a stand, it is easy to appear wishy-washy. Since the choice often leads us to act softly and with concern for our fellow man, it can give the impression that we are fearful of confrontation and are seeking the path of least resistance.

Take the ethical approach boldly and decisively. The more forthright we are in seeking the path of righteousness, the easier it will become and the more readily it will be accepted and even emulated by others. Will you have the courage to be this witness in the workplace? The Lord has called you to serve in your secular vocation. Respond with words from the refrain of a familiar hymn, "Here am I. Send me, send me!"[3]

Do not Preserve Faith - Faith sustains good works

In accordance w/ Civintegen Col 2:16,

QUESTIONS FOR DISCUSSION

1. Think of prominent examples of Christian leaders in our society. What makes them effective? What personality traits do they exhibit? How do their characteristics reflect the fruit of the Spirit? See Galatians 5:22–33. Can non-believers exhibit similar characteristics? How do you know <u>true</u> spiritual fruit?

God about God
Matt 19:17
Flow From the Spirit
Rom 13: 8-10,
Mat 22:37-40
· Acceptable
2 Cor. 4: 3-4,12
Ps 110:3

2. Suppose you were a worker in a fast-food restaurant. You observe that a young co-worker is regularly and deliberately undercharging his many friends who come in every day. Management is unaware of these actions. What should you do? What does Ephesians 4:15 say? How about Matthew 18:15–17?

? 1418-151
? ,
8th commandment

3. A talented new manager in your organization continuously speaks disparagingly about the work habits of another manager with whom she is competing for promotion. She takes every opportunity to paint her rival in a bad light. She asks you (the database administrator—a staff position) for production statistics on her rival's department. You suspect she is gathering them to present disappointing results of her rival to management. Should you give her the information, and should you voice

your concerns in any way? How might Matthew 5:43–48 guide your conversation with her? Can you be perfect? Who was perfect for you?

4. A government agency, under regulations it has written, requires a massive and detailed report to be filed on certain environmental practices by area businesses. The information requested has no apparent relation to any real environmental threat. The gathering of the data will be very burdensome. It is well known in business circles that the report is merely filed in some bureaucrat's drawer and never again consulted. You can satisfy the agency by filing a cursory answer and certify that you have used the required procedure to gather information (even though you really have not). No one will be the wiser. You simply do not have time to follow the procedures. Should you take the short cut? How does Colossians 3:22–4:1 address this concern?

CASE PROBLEMS

▶ *Competing with the Company's Customers*

Principal Characters:

Bill Hudson, counter salesman for plumbing supply store

Reggie Thorgood, sales manager

Jim Orline, company president

Susan Jackson, owner of A-1 Plumbing Contractors

THE SITUATION

Bill Hudson has sold plumbing supplies to area contractors over the counter at Acme Plumbing Supply Company for 10 years. The company sells exclusively wholesale to the trade and works at developing good relationships with the various contractor organizations. Bill is paid on an hourly basis and always gives his best effort to his job.

Since Bill has five children and a wife to support, he is always looking for means of making extra income. Having become quite knowledgeable about plumbing problems and equipment during his tenure at Acme, he began to do small plumbing jobs for friends and family on weekends and evenings. Through word-of-mouth his part-time business is beginning to grow. He buys his material from Acme using his employee discount.

As Bill's contracting business expands, he begins to quote bigger and bigger jobs. He employs a couple of helpers, who are also warehousemen at Acme. Everything seems to be going along fine until he starts bidding new home plumbing installations for a custom builder who is a fellow church member. He wins a bid for a job against A-1 Plumbing Contractors, who happen to be a regular customer of Acme Supply.

When A-1 loses the job to this unknown newcomer, A-1's owner, Sue Jackson, investigates and is outraged to find that the winning bidder is Bill Hudson's company. Sue's employees come in to Acme almost every day and buy parts and supplies from Bill Hudson.

She calls Acme sales manager Reggie Thorgood and complains about what she considers unfair competition. She says if Acme doesn't order Hudson to get out of the contracting business immediately, she will stop purchasing from Acme and notify all the local contractor organizations.

Company owner Jim Orline and sales manager Thorgood call Hudson in and tell him he must stop his side business and apologize to Ms. Jackson. They had not been aware of this side enterprise. Bill has become dependent on this extra income and feels quite strongly that what he does with his free time is his own business. Besides, many of the company's major customers started this way, with someone moonlighting a small business. Bill does not tell Orline and Thorgood that his two employees are also working at Acme. In order to save his job, Bill agrees to stop contracting. Unbeknownst to his employers, however, the two warehouse workers will continue the work, with Bill getting a percentage. Bill justifies this because he feels it is a free country and his employers have no right to infringe on the use of his free time.

QUESTIONS FOR CASE PROBLEM

1. Identify the primary ethical issues in this situation.
2. What alternatives might be open to Bill Hudson? How could he structure his part-time business without being disloyal to the interests of his employer?
3. If you were Bill Hudson, what would you do, and

why? How does this parallel Jesus' parable in Luke 16:1–13? What do we learn from it?

◗ *Moving to a Competitor*

Principal Characters:

Pam Green, product manager, Johnson's Tool Products

Harvey Connor, sales manager, Connor Tool Specialties, Inc.

Pat Brown, owner, Johnson's Tool Products

THE SITUATION

Pam Green has been a loyal employee of Johnson's Tool Products for six years. She purchases raw materials for the manufacturing line, consults regularly with the design engineers, and is in regular telephone contact with the company's key customers, who rely on her to meet their specialized custom tool needs. She has a thorough knowledge of the company's manufacturing techniques, having participated in an extensive number of seminars put on by Johnson's engineers. Many people consider her the key to the company's success, since she is at the hub of most activities and does a conscientious job.

Pam was hired straight out of school at a modest wage and has received regular, though not spectacular, raises each year. New employees recruited by the company have been paid significantly more than Pam, even though they do not have nearly her level of responsibility and skill. She is aware of this and is becoming resentful of what she feels is unfair treatment.

One night Pam is called at home by Harvey Connor who is the owner and sales manager of competitor Connor Tool Specialties. Harvey says he has heard that she is dissatisfied with her employment and offers her a position at twice the salary. They discuss the knowledge about Johnson's processes that Pam could bring, as well as her knowledge of suppliers and raw material prices. Further, she would be expected to utilize her contacts with Johnson's customers to bring them along to Connor. Harvey suggests that, prior to giving notice to her present employer, Pam should get a complete resale price list and a list of customer names and addresses at Johnson. Harvey also asks her to approach one other key employee to see if there is any interest in coming to work for Connor. If Pam and this other key employee move, then Harvey believes it will deliver a devastating blow to Johnson's business and he will pick up most of the lost business.

Pam spends two weeks getting this information before she gives her notice to Johnson's owner, Pat Brown. Brown is surprised and immediately tells Pam that they had planned to give her a large raise and a new title as vice president, but had not yet gotten around to doing it. He makes the offer now if she will stay. She accepts and agrees to stay, but that night she calls Harvey to tell him what has transpired and asks him what he wants to do about it. Harvey raises his offer to Pam by 10 percent, conditional upon delivery of the pricing and customer information within 24 hours. He points out that if Johnson Products really valued Pam, they would have taken care of her before being forced to by a competitive offer.

QUESTIONS FOR CASE PROBLEM

1. Identify the primary ethical issues in this situation.

2. Under what circumstances is it appropriate to take a job at a competing company? Are there circumstances where it would not be ethical to move to a competitor?

3. (a) Are there any ethical problems in "shopping" offers, as Pam did between the two companies? (b) What about gathering information to give to your new employer while still on the original employer's payroll?

4. What do you think about Harvey Connor's actions in setting up the proposal? Is this just good, aggressive business?

5. What should Pam do now? How does this relate to the parable of the two sons in Matthew 21:28–32?

▶ *Personal Errands*

Principal Characters:

Tom Adkinson, customer service manager, Klug's Department Store catalog division

Jeannie Fitzgerald, store general manager

THE SITUATION

Tom Adkinson is customer service manager for the catalog department of Klug's Department Store in a shopping center in a medium-sized West Coast city. He has been with the store for three years and supervises a rotating staff of 12 customer service reps. They require fairly close supervision, and his personal presence is usually required to make things run smoothly.

Tom is a single father with custody of his two teenage children. One of the children has a handicap that requires special therapy and periodic visits to the doctor. For the first two years of his employment at Klug's the company and the store manager were very tolerant of Tom's periodic absences to take the child to medical care, even though it occasionally meant service suffered in the catalog department. In the past year, however, new general manager Jeannie Fitzgerald has introduced a tough, businesslike regimen to the store. She has made it clear that she will not tolerate excessive absenteeism and that her salaried supervisors are expected to put in long hours to help meet sales goals she has set. Employees are to be part of the team or make plans to go elsewhere.

Unemployment in the city is high owing to the recent closure of several factories. Tom needs his job and the medical insurance it provides for his child. Tom begins inventing business errands he must attend to for the department just so he has an excuse to leave the premises to take his child to the doctor. His sympathetic employees know what is going on, but they cover for him. In the meantime Jeannie has instituted a sales quota for each customer service rep. One of Tom's workers who has been covering his paperwork during his frequent absences is unable to take as many customer requests as before, and her sales total is down. Jeannie studies the computer printout and instructs Tom to place this worker on probation because she is failing to meet quota.

QUESTIONS FOR CASE PROBLEM

1. What are the primary ethical issues involved here?

2. If you were company president of Klug's and you became aware of this situation, what action would you take?

3. What obligation do Tom's customer service workers have? Are they right to help him cover his absences?

4. Does Jeannie have an obligation to adopt family-flexible policies, or is she just being a good businessperson to demand compliance with policies?

5. If you were Tom, what would you do now? What might Galatians 5:13–18 say about our responsibility to live ethically? Does it allow wrong behavior? What is "loving" in this case?

◗ *The Irritating Co-worker*

Principal Characters:

Ruth Barand, accounting clerk, Anderson Publishing Company

John Davison, accounting clerk

Linda Sanders, accounting clerk

THE SITUATION

Ruth Barand is an accounting clerk for Anderson Publishing Company. She is reasonably proficient at her job, but has a problem with social adjustment at work. She is ill at ease among her co-workers and often makes inappropriate comments in an attempt to be humorous and one of the gang. She sometimes talks to herself as she does her work. This causes snickers among the workers in adjacent cubicles. One person in particular, a young man named John Davison, has begun to imitate Ruth's mannerisms in a mocking way when the group is gathered at coffee breaks. Everyone chuckles as he mimics "Crazy Ruth." Ruth appears to be unaware of what is going on behind her back, though the laughter stops and everyone is silent when she walks into the break room.

Linda Sanders, another person in the department, is present when John makes his comments. She is very uncomfortable with what she considers cruel behavior. She is a new employee, however, and is hesitant to criticize John or the others for fear of being ostracized by the group.

Ruth's behavior is getting more and more bizarre. Strangely, Linda knows someone who is a member of Ruth's church who expresses surprise at what Linda sees. She knows Ruth as a self-confident person who is well-liked at the church. Troubled by what is going on, Linda quietly approaches the department head to talk about this problem.

The department manager tells Linda that the personal relationships of the office workers are not his concern or responsibility. All he cares about is making sure the work gets out on time. He suggests Linda mind her own business and concentrate on her work. The company is large and has a human resources department. Linda considers taking this problem to the human resources director but fears that the department manager will be angry if she goes around him. In the meantime, she sees Ruth becoming more and more isolated.

QUESTIONS FOR CASE PROBLEM

1. What are the primary ethical issues involved?
2. Why might Ruth act one way at church and another way at the office?
3. What do you think of the department manager's hands-off policy concerning employee relationship problems?
4. Should Linda go to human resources with this problem, or is there another way to deal with it?
5. Sometimes it is said that certain people, by their behavior, bring the group's condemnation upon themselves. Are there some behaviors that justify this kind of ostracism? What would they be? How might Psalm 82:3–4 address this issue? How has Jesus done this for us? See Romans 5:6–8.

NOTES

1. James L. Truesdell, *Total Quality Management: Reports from the Front Line* (St. Louis: Smith-Collins Company, 1994), 146.

2. Charles Dickens, *A Christmas Carol* (St. Louis: MCE Publishing Co., 1996), 93.

3. "Hark, the Voice of Jesus Calling," from *Lutheran Worship* 318. Text: Daniel March 1819–1909, alt.

◆

6

Putting It All Together

JAMES L. TRUESDELL

God has given us grace and forgiveness through Jesus Christ. We are saved by faith and have eternal life. That is His plan of salvation. Shouldn't we then have a plan for living so that we give Him glory? "When I planned this, did I do it lightly? Or do I make my plans in a worldly manner" (2 Corinthians 1:17).

One of the central tenets of management is that if you want to achieve a goal, you must have a plan. If the goal is financial, such as profit or sales, a specific numerical goal can and should be set. If you do not set a specific profit goal, then you are merely hoping that something will be left over for profit. So it is with your working life. If you do not construct a plan for meeting the challenges of your job in a Christian fashion, you may be taking care of all the other needs of the world first and just hoping there is time, effort, and thought left over for God. Bringing God into your working life can be made easier by taking some specific steps:

1. Recognize that your work is your vocation and that you are called by God to serve Him there.

2. Address ethical decisions in a systematic way to ensure that you listen to your conscience, defining how the Lord would have you act in any given situation.

3. Develop a personal mission statement to guide your daily interactions with others and to build your faith life.

4. Ensure that your priorities are set on God and caring for your fellow man.

5. Readily and willingly forgive those who have transgressed against you and humbly ask God's forgiveness for your own shortcomings.

WORK AS A VOCATION

In medieval times there was a distinct line between clerics, who devoted their lives to God, and everyone else. You either devoted yourself to God totally or you slogged your way through the mire of the world, taking your inspiration from those holy men who spent their lives in prayer and meditation.[1] A pastor once noted the difference in two congregations he had served: "In my current congregation the parishioners want me to teach *them* how to live good lives and be people of faith. In my first church the people wanted *me* to be good so they could feel good about having a holy man as pastor."

Therein lies the challenge to us. We cannot dismiss

our faith as applicable only to our church life. Neither can we see only those in full-time church work as capable of or obligated to live their beliefs in the nine-to-five working world. This was clearly understood by Martin Luther, who espoused the concept of all work as a vocation. He taught that each of us has a duty to do our job well as a way to serve God. This applies regardless of one's station or occupation.[2] We as Christians are called to be engaged in the world, as witnesses to the Gospel through the service we perform for others and through the example of ethical choices we make. These are an expression of our gratitude for God's grace through Christ. This sets us apart from those who may make the same ethical choices, but do so for other reasons—because "ethics is good business," because of fear of breaking the law or of being held to the light of public scrutiny, or even from sincerely held humanistic beliefs in right and wrong.

Whether or not you love your job, you can begin to see it as a calling in which you can witness through service and example. Look for ways to solve someone's problems, to ease someone's burden, to soften conflict, or to improve the quality of life for your customers or co-workers. Help mold your company's mission and work practices to be consistent with what you believe is God's will based on your regular reading of God's Word. Seek guidance in regular daily prayer. Find others within your work group or profession with whom you can have Christian fellowship. "But Jesus often withdrew to lonely places and prayed" (Luke 5:16). "For where two or three come together in My name, there am I with them" (Matthew 18:20).

SEEKING GOD'S WILL IN ETHICAL CHOICES

In an earlier chapter we examined a series of applied tests for ethical decision-making. These are the legal/compliance test, the public knowledge test, the long-term consequences test, the examine-your-motives test, and the inner voice test. This last is our conscience, shaped and guided by the written Word of God. While the first four tests can help us in providing a framework for our decision, it is this last that we must heed if we are to be at peace with ourselves.

It is indeed God's will we seek and not our own. Neither do we substitute ourselves for God by devising our own moral code. If our inner voice is to reflect God's will, then we must possess a solid foundation in the Word. In that way we reflect the Ten Commandments and follow Christ's example and teaching in dealing with daily situations.

As parents we can raise our children in the knowledge of the Lord with regular participation in church and family devotions. Give your children the foundation and set a personal example for them so that, when confronted with difficult situations as working adults, their inner voice will speak clearly and loudly to them. Even if you have not had a Christian upbringing, you can, through study of God's Word and being discipled by those who are mature in their faith, gain the resources and spiritual underpinnings to guide you in the right path.

Strengthened by the Word, we trust in the Lord, seeking His guidance in prayer and asking for strength to resist temptation. Since we are weak in the flesh, we should avoid situations that place temptation before us. Seek business associates who are men and women of integrity. Avoid dealing with those who skate the edges of morality. We know that we must deal with those in the world who will prey upon us or entice us to step over the line. We are exhorted by Scripture to defend ourselves against temptation.

> Put on the full armor of God so that you can take your stand against the devil's schemes. For our struggle is not against flesh and blood, but against the rulers, against the authorities, against the powers of this dark world and against the spiritual forces of evil in the heavenly realms. Therefore put on the full armor of God, so that when the day of evil comes, you may be able to stand your ground, and after you have done everything, to stand. Stand firm then, with the belt of truth buckled around your waist, with the breastplate of righteousness in place, and with your feet fitted with the readiness that comes from the gospel of peace. In addition to all this, take up the shield of faith, with which you can extinguish all the flaming arrows of the evil one. Take the helmet

of salvation and the sword of the Spirit, which
is the word of God. (Ephesians 6:11–17)

This reminds us that we are <u>engaged in spiritual
warfare</u> against the forces of darkness. The Holy Spirit
working through the Word and Sacraments equips us
with armor and weapons to win this struggle. We put
on the armor of God when we grow in the Christian
faith. Having been strengthened in faith, we make wise
choices in our home and work lives, steeped in prayer
and the study of the Word.

DEVELOPING A PERSONAL
MISSION STATEMENT

Effective organizations have a clear sense of mission. The leadership clearly and cogently articulates the
prime focus of the enterprise. Strategic plans and allo-
cation of resources then logically flow so as to accomplish that mission. Can we apply the same concept to
our lives as Christians? A personal mission statement
can define how to budget time, how to be effective in
church and at work, and how to approach relationships
at work and home.

The concept of a personal mission statement for the
Christian businessperson was expanded upon by Mark
Dunlop, who worked with us in our 1997 seminar on
Christian Ethics in the Workplace. Mark is director of
Worker Benefit Plans member services for The Lutheran
Church—Missouri Synod. According to Dunlop, a mis-

sion statement is like a net under a tightrope that catches you and helps you get back on track in utilizing the gifts that God has given you. The mission statement can help in budgeting time for devotions, exercise, family, and extended family time so there can be balance between God, family, and self. It provides a way to use the time and talents God has given us in an effective way.

What should guide us as we develop a mission statement? A Lutheran Laymen's League workshop suggested getting the "P's" straight:

Pursue God over goals.

Prefer people over plans.

Predicate any activity by asking, "What does love demand?"

Our normal human inclination is to gravitate to power—to revel in acquiring it for ourselves. But in defining our Christian mission, we must ask whether we are willing to sacrifice authority for love. We do not ask what our position, power, or authority permit us to do. We do not ask what our reciprocal obligations or strategies require us to do. We do not ask what will please everyone the most. We do not ask what will edify us or meet the expectations of our organizations or our superiors.

Rather than looking at things from the above perspectives, we ask the following:

1. Do my co-workers/subordinates/peers—or even my children—imitate me as a Christian? Can they see Christ in me?

2. What characteristics can I see in them that they got from me?

3. What is the most important aspect of my faith that I hope to give them?

4. What character traits did I learn from a Christian role model in my life?

5. How can I encourage others in the faith and be a role model for them?

6. What traits do I have that I wish to leave at the cross?

7. How can I be prepared to give a witness in all situations? See 1 Peter 3:13-18a.

Answering these questions can help us focus on what is really important in our lives and our relationships. From there we can construct our mission statement to help us move in the direction of truly living our faith. The statement should not only define our goal but also move us toward action. Here is an example of such a statement, as developed by Mark Dunlop: "All that I do is ultimately to have a positive impact on others. This is primarily to include my family, my fellow believers, my employer, my clients, my co-workers, and those with whom I have the opportunity to meet and interact. It is my ultimate hope that other people and I will have a relationship to God and will grow in that relationship. My life is to be an example of how Christ can work through man." [3]

We each must develop our own statement—one that speaks to our own particular situation, needs, and goals. Perhaps you will want to discuss this with other

Christian friends who can provide support and accountability in living your mission.

KEEPING OUR PRIORITIES STRAIGHT

Many of those who counsel people on financial and career planning say that to become rich or powerful you must make that your constant and consuming goal. You must keep that goal in the forefront of your mind and continuously monitor your progress toward achieving it. That may or may not work, but even if it did, would such a focus bring us happiness or contentment? Likely it would not. "For where your treasure is, there your heart will be also" (Matthew 6:21).

If we focus on amassing riches or acquiring power, that will be the desire of our heart and there will be little room for God or others. We make choices about what our priorities will be and where we will invest our thoughts, time, and efforts. "But seek first His kingdom and His righteousness, and all these things will be given to you as well" (Matthew 6:33).

As God's children we are given many gifts and talents. We honor our Lord by utilizing these gifts to the fullest—working hard to provide for our family and providing services and goods for others as a part of the wonderful world God has given us. If we see our efforts in this perspective, honoring Him rather than glorifying ourselves, then we approach our jobs with the correct priorities. If our talents and gifts then lead us to material success or to the top of our profession or to the position of CEO of our company, we will see it as an opportunity for service and not use our position to dominate or abuse others.

GIVING AND SEEKING FORGIVENESS

Because the working world is often full of strife, competition, and conflict, it is easy to hold anger in your heart toward someone—a competitor, a supervisor, a rival, or almost anyone whom you feel has unfairly thwarted your efforts or plans. When you hold a grudge it diminishes your ability to carry out your work effectively. It becomes hard to form good relationships at home and work. Envy robs you of energy and inner peace. You have received grace and forgiveness through Christ's sacrifice, so express your thanks by forgiving others. This can be hard when others do not believe they need forgiveness and see nothing wrong in their actions, but that does not relieve you of the obligation to forgive them for Christ's sake. Opening your heart in such a way prepares you to forthrightly lay your own sins, bad thoughts, and shortcomings at the foot of the cross. "For if you forgive men when they sin against you, your heavenly Father will also forgive you. But if you do not forgive men their sins, your Father will not forgive your sins" (Matthew 6:14–15).

Do you sometimes find it hard to get up and face each new day in the workplace? Do you find yourself beset by feelings of anger, frustration, and inadequacy in your job? Let it all go and place your cares and concerns in God's hands.

REACHING OUT TO OTHERS

Christ came that we may have life and have it to the full (John 10:10). That fullness can be a part of all of your life, even when you are focused on earning a living and performing the mundane tasks that are part of every job. This holds true even when you compete for sales, make tough decisions that adversely affect others, or spend hours in physical labor. Your work life is a calling to serve others and let your light of faith shine as a witness to others. You can act boldly and decisively to make positive choices when confronted with the opportunity—and you can live by a plan, a mission—that will keep you focused on your true calling.

James Dobson, in his Focus on the Family series, once said that the most important challenge in one's life is to "Be there (in heaven)! And take as many people as you can with you."[4] Make every day in the workplace a testimony to your faith in Christ and an invitation by your actions for others to join you!

NOTES

1. Oliver Williams and John Houck, eds., *The Judeo-Christian Vision and the Modern Corporation* (Notre Dame: Notre Dame University Press, 1982), 9–10.

2. James M. Childs, Jr., *Ethics in Business: Faith at Work* (Minneapolis: Augsburg Fortress, 1995), 21–23.

3. From presentation notes of Mark Dunlop from seminar on Christian Ethics in the Workplace at St. Paul Lutheran Church, Des Peres, Missouri, 1997.

4. James Dobson, *Life on the Edge: Preparing for the Challenges of Adulthood* (Waco: Word Publishing, 1993), videotape.

◆